PUERTO RICANS

By Petra Press

BENCHMARK BOOKS

MARSHALL CAVENDISH

Benchmark Books
Marshall Cavendish Corporation
99 White Plains Road
Tarrytown, New York 10591-9001, U.S.A.

© Marshall Cavendish Corporation, 1996

Edited, designed, and produced by Water Buffalo Books, Milwaukee

Editorial consultant: Manuel Santiago-Soto, Coordinator of Multicultural Programs, Marquette University

Picture Credits: Sabine Beaupré 1995: 7, 21; © The Bettmann Archive: 10, 11, 14, 16, 19; © Beryl Goldberg: 6, 32, 34,
40, 46, 55; © Hazel Hankin: Cover, 5, 30, 35, 38, 47 (top), 51; © Antonio Pérez/¡Exito!: 28, 36, 65; © Paul M. Perez: 1,
39, 42; © Reuters/Bettmann: 62, 68; © Katrina Thomas: 4, 45, 47 (bottom), 48, 52, 54, 59, 60, 61, 75; ©
UPI/Bettmann: 13, 20, 24, 26, 27, 63, 69, 70 (both), 72 (both), 73

Library of Congress Cataloging-in-Publication Data

Press, Petra.
     Puerto Rican Americans / by Petra Press.
          p.   cm. -- (Cultures of America)
     Includes bibliographical references and index.
     ISBN 0-7614-0160-1 (lib. bdg.)
     1. Puerto Ricans--United States--Juvenile literature. 2. Puerto Rico--Juvenile literature. I. Title.
E184.P85P74   1995   95-11054
973'.04687295--dc20   CIP
                                                                    AC

To PS – MS

Printed in Malaysia
Bound in the U.S.A.

CONTENTS

INTRODUCTION

Of all the ethnic groups that have become part of the United States, few have a cultural history and set of traditions as rich and complex as those of Puerto Ricans. Just about all facets of Puerto Rican life — food, music, art, religion, dress, architecture, sense of family and community — are touched by a mix of Spanish, Taino Indian, and African influences, with traditions that often go back four hundred years or more.

Puerto Rican migration to the mainland has been distinctive in many respects. Unlike most ethnic groups, Puerto Ricans were U.S. citizens before they ever even reached the mainland. Puerto Ricans living on the island of Puerto Rico are also the first U.S. citizens to debate the possibility of independence. The large numbers of Puerto Ricans who migrated to the mainland after World War II became the first immigrant groups to arrive by plane, and they continue to travel back and forth from their homeland at a much higher rate than any other immigrant group. They also did not readily give up their language, religion, and other cultural traditions to assimilate into the great Anglo "melting pot," despite tremendous pressures to do so. Yet even as they struggled hard to overcome prejudice, economic inequality, and discrimination (a fight that continues in many areas even today), they never stopped enriching U.S. culture with their art, music, literature, theater, language, food, family values, personal dignity, and celebration of faith.

The 1990 U.S. census showed that almost 2.5 million Puerto Ricans live on the U.S. mainland, with another 3.5 million making their home on the island. In this book, you will learn about the ways in which Puerto Ricans have distinguished themselves as members of a unique American culture — a group that has kept its distinct cultural identity even as its tremendous contributions have expanded every facet of American life from opera and poetry to MTV, from business, science, and politics to movies and baseball.

From sun-drenched, sandy ocean fronts like Luquillo Beach (twenty-five miles east of San Juan) to the lush mountain foliage of the island's interior, Puerto Rico is truly a tropical island paradise.

CHAPTER ONE

LEAVING A HOMELAND
PUERTO RICO'S SPECIAL NATIONAL BLEND

On a warm summer evening in the early 1900s, a few years after the island had become a U.S. possession and farming jobs were becoming scarce, Tomás Vega looked with sadness at his two small children sleeping so peacefully in their corner of the bedroom. Tomorrow morning he would have to leave his house in the hills again, this time for the *zafra*, the cane harvest on the other side of the island, and it would be at least six weeks before he would see his family again. He tucked the blanket more snugly around his son and kissed his baby daughter lightly on the forehead, quietly so he would not wake them up. Tomás did not mind the backbreaking work or even the low pay; he gladly worked hard to support his wife and growing family. What was hard for him to take was being separated from them for so many months at a time.

Some men in town were talking about a new schoolhouse scheduled to be built in the spring, which meant that when Tomás returned, he might have a well-paying construction job that was actually close to home. But he knew better than to count on it. Even if the talk were true, there were so many other men in his *barrio* (village) looking for work — most with families larger than his — that his chances of getting hired on the temporary construction crew were not that good. But that's the way things were and one had to make the best of it, he thought to himself, quietly closing the bedroom door and joining his wife in the kitchen. And tonight is not a night to be sad! All the women in the family had been cooking his favorites all day — *lechón asado* (roast pork), *pasteles,* and *asopao* — for a party in his honor, and his parents' house would be alive with laughter and dancing till long after midnight. Tomás hugged his wife and silently thanked the saints for his beautiful family.

The Caribbean island of Puerto Rico is 38 miles wide and 111 miles long and has a range of low mountains stretching like a backbone through the center. The tropical island has a pleasant climate with a year-round average temperature of seventy-five degrees — but it also lies right in the middle of the Atlantic Ocean's major hurricane path, causing it to get hit occasionally with devastating storms.

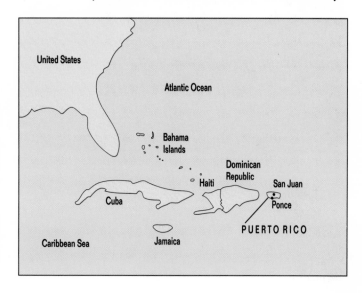

A Rich Spanish, African, and Indian Heritage

Puerto Rico's unique culture has been nourished by indigenous, European, African, and North American influences. There are, for example, no typical "Puerto Rican" characteristics. Some Puerto Ricans have straight dark hair, brown skin, and dark eyes — features that can be traced back to indigenous Taino ancestors, the Indians who inhabited the island since before Spanish colonists arrived in the early 1500s. Many Puerto Ricans have African skin tones and facial features. These characteristics may be traced back to African ancestors who eventually freed themselves from slavery after the Spanish brought them to the island in the sixteenth and seventeenth centuries. Others have fair skin and green eyes inherited from Spanish ancestors. Still others have reddish blonde hair handed down from the Irish and other European immigrants who settled on the island in the nineteenth century.

Since the end of the sixteenth century, Taino and African inhabitants have intermarried with Spanish and other Europeans, as well as with each other, producing a wide variation within the same family. By the late nineteenth century, few Puerto Rican families were all European, all Indian, or all Black, but instead a mixture of the three. Most Puerto Ricans today thus have some sort of combination of these physical features. These roots may be found in almost every part of Puerto Rico's rich culture: food, music, art, religion, dress, architecture, farming, even courtship rituals.

The main European influences on Puerto Rican life during the eighteenth and nineteenth centuries were Catholicism, the Spanish language, and a feudal agricultural system. In this type of land system, rural areas were primarily large farms (*haciendas*) owned by wealthy landowners (*patrónes*), and farmed by generation after generation of poor landless tenants (*agregados* or *jíbaros*) who lived with their fam-

THE HIGH PRICE OF GOLD

The Taino were a peaceful group of Arawakan Indians with a highly developed Caribbean culture based on agriculture, fishing, and hunting sea mammals. Taino communities typically consisted of multifamily households that held as many as fifty people each. Because of the warm climate, the Taino did not have to build elaborate housing or spend a lot of time searching for food. This left them with the leisure time to design and make superbly crafted pottery, baskets, woven cotton cloth, and elaborate stone sculptures.

There were over thirty thousand Taino Indians living on the island of Puer-

to Rico before Christopher Columbus landed on his second voyage to the Americas in 1493. Gold-seeking Spanish colonists severely reduced both the number of the island's inhabitants and its mineral resources in just a few short decades. The Spanish used Taino men, women, and children as slave labor, first in the mines, then on their sugar plantations. By 1514 (only twenty-two years later), there were only four thousand Taino left; by 1530, fewer than twelve hundred. Those who did not die from harsh treatment and overwork died from epidemic diseases the Spanish brought from Europe.

UNWILLING AFRICAN IMMIGRANTS

The Spaniards introduced sugar cane to the island in 1511 and made it the primary focus of their exploitation after they had exhausted the island's gold mines. When they started running out of Indian slaves to work the sugar cane plantations, they simply imported African replacements. The first Black slaves arrived in 1518, and by 1530, Africans outnumbered both Spaniards and Taino Indians. Unlike the Indians, however, Black slaves had the legal right in Puerto Rico to marry, own property, and eventually buy their freedom. They were also treated far less cruelly. Although slavery was not officially abolished on the island until 1873, many slaves either bought their freedom or were freed by their owners during the eighteenth and nineteenth centuries. By 1800, there were as many free Blacks on the island as there were Black slaves. Africans added a rich new dimension to the Spanish-Taino culture and affected the development of all facets of Puerto Rican life, including language, religion, music, art, and cuisine.

ilies in shacks around the landowner's house. Men did most of the heavier farm work, but besides helping the landowner's wife with all of her household chores, women and children had to help with crop planting and harvesting as well. The *jíbaros* were usually *mestizos* (people of mixed Spanish and Taino blood), *mulattos* (people of mixed Spanish and African blood), or *zambos* (descendants of African-Indian marriages).

The feudal landlord-tenant system may have left the *jíbaros* poor and propertyless, but it did have certain advantages. Jíbaro families stayed on the same hacienda for generations, and the patrón and his wife usually took a personal interest in their laborers' families and looked out for their welfare. They treated their tenants fairly and with respect, making sure they had medical care when they needed it and often even becoming godparents to their workers' children. The workers, in turn, gave the patrón's family their loyalty. The system was rooted in values of dignity and respect for everyone by everyone — rich and poor alike.

The introduction of Africans into Puerto Rican culture had a major influence on the family unit. As Blacks, whites, and mestizos married one another, people within the same family often had a variety of different skin shades. Because color defined social status, different members of the same family could actually belong to different social classes and be treated accordingly. (The darkest person in the family was usually called *"el negro."*)

The Spanish imported Black slaves to work the coastal sugar plantations. As a result, even after they were freed, families of African descent tended to stay in coastal areas, and jíbaros continued to work on the inland haciendas.

More Change: U.S. Rule

U.S. occupation of the island also brought major cultural changes. Puerto Rico became a U.S. territory when Spain was forced to cede the colony in 1898 after the Spanish-American War. For a two-year period after that, the island was occupied and ruled by U.S. military forces. U.S. occupation brought about both desirable and not-so-desirable changes to Puerto Rican family and community life. On the positive side: The U.S. forces helped build roads, schools, sewer systems, and public housing. But there were devastating negative effects of the U.S. occupation as well. It destroyed much of the island's culture and traditions, exploited the work force and created even more devastating poverty, undermined traditional family values by breaking apart extended families and undermining strict parental authority, and created a great deal of resentment.

Living in a Rural Society

During the time Spain had ruled the island, from the 1500s to the time the United States took over in 1898, every rural community or *pueblo* was formed in the same way and patterned after the Catholic towns Spanish colonists had left behind in Spain. The town plaza was the center of the community life, the place where all members of the community could meet, celebrate fiestas, and participate in religious ceremonies. The main building on the plaza was always the Catholic church because people believed that no community could exist until God was a member of it.

People lived in small wood or wood-and-cement houses called *bohios* that usually had only one or two sparsely furnished rooms besides the kitchen with its kerosene stove and shelves containing the family's few pots and dishes. No matter how poor a family was, however, the wife took pains to be a good housekeeper, and guests were always welcome. Many houses were decorated with pictures of saints; many also had small altars in honor of a particular patron saint.

Extended families (grandparents, aunts, uncles, cousins) always lived in close proximity to each other, sometimes in the same house if the building was large enough. Sosme houses had their own access to a well, but usually a group of houses shared access, and women had to carry the water they needed to their individual homes.

In the early 1900s, peasant families often lived in makeshift beach huts as they migrated throughout the island in search of temporary work on fishing crews or coconut plantations.

In the early 1900s, U.S. farming technology eliminated the need for many full-time workers, forcing families like this one harvesting grapefruit on a plantation outside of San Juan to become migrants constantly in search of temporary work.

Rural Life Under U.S. Rule

When the United States arrived in 1898, occupation also meant industrialization, a change that had a profound effect on every aspect of Puerto Rican life, but perhaps most drastically on the way rural peasants made a living. Until that time, large, family-owned haciendas grew sugar cane on the fertile coastal plains. Further inland, on less fertile land in the hills, haciendas grew other crops such as tobacco, coffee, and various kinds of fruit. When the United States took over the island, most of the sugar cane haciendas were given to mainland corporations, which immediately turned the growing of sugar cane into a highly profitable industry. To make the sugar fields as efficient as possible, the corporations uprooted the tenant, or jíbaros, families who had worked the haciendas for generations and took over their small plots of land.

Families either became squatters on unfarmable land up in the mountains or started moving in search of work. For many, moving, often from community, to community became a way of life. Not only were men out of the farming jobs that had been guaranteed to them by the patrón families for generations, but their families no longer even had the small plots of land on which they could grow vegetables to survive. Jíbaros had no other skills and, for the first time in their lives, no support from anyone. Even the families working the inland coconut, tobacco, and coffee plantations were threatened because U.S. competition made these haciendas less profitable. Many owners had to cut back to temporary and seasonal employees instead of employing jíbaro families who permanently lived on the premises.

So the beginning of the twentieth century saw Puerto Rican peasants start to move all over the island in search of jobs. Fathers either left home or traveled with their families and meager belongings. Young teenagers living on tobacco and coffee plantations left home in hopes the cities' factories would offer them better work opportunities. Even women started getting industrial jobs where they were available to help contribute to family income.

At the same time, the population began to boom, making the competition for both country and city jobs even more fierce. Many families had to move every few months in search of work because whatever work they found was either seasonal (like harvesting cane) or short-term (like laboring on municipal construction projects).

A number of different jobs were available to unskilled workers. Sugar cane was by far the most important seasonal cash crop on the island, but there were many inland fruit, coconut, and coffee plantations as well. There was also factory work. In addition to processing sugar cane, factories produced hundreds of different items — everything from canned food to leather wallets. There were also fishing cooperatives and construction companies that hired temporary or part-time help.

Whether they stayed in one rural community or kept moving, most family breadwinners had to hold down at least three or four different jobs a year just to feed their families. A man, for example, would sign up to work the cane fields from February through July, gather coconuts for a nearby coconut plantation until mid-September, work the *zafra* (cane harvest) for a few weeks, then fish from November to early February. He might pick up a higher-paying, short-term construction job between the other work — if he was lucky. His wife might find work at the crab cannery two or three days a week, depending on the supply and quality of crabs the fishermen brought in.

Factories manufacturing clothing offered more hours and higher pay, but many women competed for those jobs and the work was hard to get. Most factories had layoff periods (usually during December and March), so even fac-

MIXED FEELINGS ABOUT BECOMING "AMERICAN"

During its two-year military occupation, the United States helped build improved schools, roads, municipal buildings, factories and sewage systems, but Puerto Ricans had strong and mixed feelings about these efforts right from the start. The United States believed its role in Puerto Rico was to "civilize" it — to bring the benefits of science, technology, and capitalism and to convert the peoples of Puerto Rico to U.S. cultural and social standards. In American eyes at the end of the nineteenth century, Puerto Rico was a backward, uncivilized country whose inhabitants were somewhat lazy and ignorant and by no means knowledgeable enough to govern themselves. Most Puerto Ricans at the end of the nineteenth century, on the other hand, did not exactly view what the United States wanted to give them as "benefits." In their eyes, the United States was a country preoccupied with producing and consuming material goods. To them, the United States was neglecting more important values, such as respect, dignity, and a less aggressive attitude toward one's neighbors. Puerto Ricans felt both ready and entitled to rule themselves and resented being an occupied U.S. territory.

HARVESTING CANE

Harvesting sugar cane — cutting cane stalks with a machete for ten hours a day under glaring sun — was one of the hardest jobs a man could get. A cane cutter worked as part of a larger squad that worked its way up and down rows of ripened cane stalks, with the faster, more efficient cutters in the front and the older, slower cutters bringing up the rear.

A cutter seizes the cane stalk with one hand and strikes it above the ground just high enough for the stump to grow new stalks in the next growing season. After stripping off the leaves, he cuts the stalk into several pieces and throws them onto a pile. Later, other workers (called loaders) pick up the stalk piles and load them into railroad dump cars or rubber-wheeled carts to be carried off to the "central" or sugar mill for processing.

At the central, the cane is dumped into a shaft to begin the refining process. In earlier times, the cane was often burned before cutting. Cutters earned time and a half for cutting burned cane, a job many workers turned down in spite of the higher pay because of the powdery substance produced by the burned cane that settled into their lungs while they were cutting it. This substance often caused a chronic condition workers called "lung infection."

tory work was available for ten months of the year at best.

Whether a person worked on a sugar plantation, stitched leather in a wallet factory, or poured cement for a construction crew, working conditions were worse after the United States took over than most Puerto Ricans had known before. Not only was the work hard, the hours long, and the pay terrible, but employees were treated more like animals than

As late as 1920, peasant laborers were so desperate for temporary work that mainland owners of island sugar plantations knew they could make tremendous profits by paying them small wages for back-breaking harvest work.

When city factory jobs became scarce, some enterprising peasants like this shoe salesman became street vendors.

In the early twentieth century, there were no unions and no union representatives to whom workers could go with complaints and no medical or other employee benefits — in short, nothing to stop managers from exploiting and insulting them. Because so many people were looking for work, managers did not think twice about simply firing anyone who complained. Many factories imposed educational requirements that included a working knowledge of English and a three-to-six-month training period during which employees were paid only a small fraction of their would-be salary. Although these jobs usually paid much more per hour than the average factory jobs, few rural peasants could speak English well enough to qualify — or afford to work for so many months without making a livable wage.

This demeaning treatment was as harsh a culture shock as being uprooted from hacienda life and forced to constantly move in search for menial employment. It is no wonder that when the U.S. Congress passed the Jones Act in 1917 and granted citizenship to every Puerto Rican who wanted it, people began to look to the U.S. mainland as a way out.

The Hard Adjustment to City Life

Within a few short years after U.S. occupation ended, the booming population and declining number of rural jobs in farming, fishing, and construction made the competition for work even more difficult. Thousands of desperate families migrated to the island's larger cities (like San Juan) in search of factory or service jobs. Even for those who found work

people. Unlike the patrónes, who at least took a personal interest in the welfare of the agregado who worked for them, the owners and managers of these new mainland-owned industries cared only about higher production. They were not interested in the safety of their employees and certainly not in treating them with respect. Nineteenth-century Puerto Rican society might have been unfairly divided into two widely separated social classes — rich landowners and poor workers — but in that society, both landowner and worker valued patience, respect, and dignity over material gain. In fact, lack of respect toward one's employees was considered not just rude, but cowardly and unmanly.

in the cities, life did not get much better. Most jíbaros had little or no education, and only a few had the skills to become artisans such as masons or carpenters. Instead, most became factory workers (many of them laid off during frequent slack periods), pick-and-shovel construction workers and longshoremen (usually part-time or temporary work), or service workers who were only employed at the height of the tourist season. Some became pushcart peddlers or ran tiny stores out of their homes.

Many jíbaro families were so poor when they reached the city that they had to sell the few belongings they had just to buy food. Those who could afford housing at all settled in the city's slum tenements; the rest took up rent-free residence in shantytowns on the city's outskirts. Slums were usually neighborhoods of old, rundown inner-city buildings dangerously overcrowded with poor families (dangerous because of the threats of fire and epidemic diseases).

Shantytowns were even worse. These were clusters of makeshift buildings on the outer edges of the city on land considered unfit even for industrial use. Families did not own or rent the land but merely "squatted" on it, and their only building materials were industrial castoffs like sheet metal and the bricks and wooden debris from wrecked buildings. These shanties were usually built along a stream or canal on piles to raise them off the mud and protect them from frequent floods. Shantytowns had no community services such as piped water, garbage collection, or a sewage system; people had no choice but to use the canal instead. (Over the years, however, many of the shantytowns did obtain police and fire protection, access to elementary schools, and some health and welfare services. Some even eventually acquired electricity and running water.)

Family Life

Whether people lived in rural areas or in the city, the family continued to be the most important social unit in Puerto Rican life. In rural communities (or on the remaining haciendas), the large number of aunts, uncles, grandparents, cousins, *compadres* (godparents or very close friends), and any other natural or ritual kin usually lived together as an extended family, either in a single household or so close by that they could constantly visit each other. Bonds between members of the extended family were very close. If people needed financial or emotional aid, a place to live if they were unemployed, or help raising their children, the extended family was always there for them.

In the country, people believed that the male was the household's most important figure and the supposedly weaker female was always secondary. Traditionally, it was the man's role to provide for and protect the family, while it was considered the woman's job to serve men, raise the children, and do the household chores. Women were not allowed to pursue a higher education, and the only careers open to women at all were teaching and religious vocations. At the same time, however, the mother enjoyed a privileged position in the family and was idolized and revered by the family.

Parents believed their children were sent to them by God and that their children were their wealth. All family members (not just the parents) did everything they could to nurture and protect them, although "for their own good," children had few rights and were strongly disciplined. Children were never left alone. It was not unusual for a child to be given permanently to another family member in the household to raise in order to protect the child's welfare (if, for example, the parents had to face the uncertainty of traveling to look for work).

Men were not the only ones who contributed to a family's income. Women, older people, and even young children wove straw hats or worked on other crafts that could be sold in the city.

Grandparents and other elderly family members often helped out with taking care of the children and were respected and revered for their wisdom and experience. If the elderly became unable to take care of themselves, the rest of the family immediately stepped in to provide the care they needed.

City families, on the other hand, were usually limited to what is called the nuclear family: the mother, father, and children. Most nuclear families moved to the city to find work, and the city was too far away to stay in close touch with their extended families. That meant they did not have the economic and emotional support to fall back on or the help in raising their children. No longer as needed, the elderly became less important and sometimes were even left behind to take care of themselves. Without other family members to watch them, older city children often had to be left alone for part of the day while both parents worked.

Nuclear city families had other stresses to deal with as well. One of the traditional ways a Puerto Rican man defined his masculinity was his ability to support his family. His wife was not supposed to work outside the house. But for families to survive the high cost of city living, both parents often had to find work. Sometimes it was easier for women to get and keep factory jobs than it was for men. In a culture that placed so much value on a man's ability to provide for his family, a working wife was often demoralizing, and the resulting conflict put a great deal of strain on many marriages. Conflicts between parents and children were also common because children attended city schools that exposed them to values and lifestyles that conflicted with those of their parents. Children were taught that they had some rights, too, and (at least in school) did not deserve to be subjected to corporal punishment. Teenagers, especially girls, started demanding fewer restrictions and more of a say in determining their futures.

Americanizing Education

Educating their children was an important goal of Puerto Rican parents, but before 1898, only a few even had the money and opportunity to send their children to elementary school. Even when they could, only the boys attended school because it was believed that girls did not need to learn more than how to run a household and raise children. Schools for boys were mostly Catholic schools run by nuns whose emphasis was usually on religious subjects. Boys were taught basic reading and arithmetic skills, mainly by the memorization method.

When the United States took over and occupied the island in 1898, one of its first goals was to reorganize schools and eliminate the island's illiteracy. It immediately made some major changes in Puerto Rico's educational policy, like admitting girls as well as boys and teaching them together in coeducational classrooms. The new educational policy also banned religious instruction in the public schools and introduced organized athletics and competitive team sports. Instead of using the memorization approach to teaching, teachers began to use problem-solving methods.

The new policy did improve the island's literacy rate. In 1900, only 14 percent of Puerto Rican children were in school and only 25 percent of the population could read and write. Forty years later, over 50 percent of all school-age children were in school and the literacy rate had climbed to 66 percent, figures that continued to climb to over 90 percent over the next five decades.

But while increased literacy was certainly an achievement, the educational policy introduced by the U.S. government had more drawbacks than benefits. First of all, the second but

equally stressed aim of the U.S. administrators of Puerto Rican school policy was Americanization. That meant eliminating the Spanish language, destroying Puerto Rican culture and heritage, and replacing it with English, U.S. history classes, and such indoctrination techniques as the daily saluting of the U.S. flag and the singing of patriotic U.S. songs. Not only were students forced to *learn* the English language, teachers were forced to use it as the language of instruction — even to students who had no prior knowledge of English at all. (In 1910, only 4 percent of the entire population could speak English.) Spanish was banned from schools entirely. It was not until 1930 that the U.S. government agreed to modify this policy to allow elementary and secondary teachers to teach in Spanish, although English was still to be taught as a required subject.

The Americanization policy caused several major problems. Both teachers and pupils resented being forced into a system that made it almost impossible for children to learn. Large numbers of students simply dropped out of school because language difficulties made classes too frustrating, and teachers were too intimidated by the political control of the schools to protest. In addition, the overall education offered on the island under U.S. rule was generally of poor quality because teachers were underpaid and poorly trained.

Another problem was the conflict between ideas children were exposed to in school and the traditional values held by their parents. The U.S. style of education promoted independence, coeducational activities, and competition, for example, while traditional Puerto Ricans valued family, cooperation, education for males only, and the sheltering and separation of girls until marriage. Stressing the inner worth of a person and values such as respect and dignity were replaced in schools by measuring a person's worth by the number of A's he or she received or the number of track medals he or she won.

Traditional values also demanded absolute obedience from one's children; the longer children attended these new schools, the less they seemed to listen to and respect their elders. Perhaps the most damaging effect of the educational policies the United States imposed was that many children, especially teens, became ashamed of their cultural heritage and felt increasingly worthless because their families were poor. In many ways, the United States caused as many problems with the educational system it introduced as it had helped to solve.

Courtship and Marriage

Unlike young people on the U.S. mainland who date each other, fall in love, and then tell their parents about their decision to marry, Puerto Rican teens were traditionally much more restricted. Girls were almost always kept separate from boys in social situations. If a young man became interested in a young woman, he was expected to ask the girl's father for permission to court her before even speaking to the girl herself. If her parents disapproved, he did not have a chance. If the parents did give their approval, the girl became the boy's *novia,* and he was allowed to visit her in her parents' home and go out on well-chaperoned dates with her. When the young couple decided to get married (assuming her parents agreed to the union), they got married in church if the parents could afford a church wedding. Poorer couples were married in civil ceremonies or without any legal ceremony at all. Even without a marriage certificate, the couple agreed to live together for life as husband and wife and raise their children. Traditionally, a new wife was expected to give birth to her first child within a year of her marriage.

These traditional values did not carry over well into the city. Girls were already mixing socially with boys as early as elementary school, and when they became teenagers, they demanded to go out on dates without being chaperoned. They also wanted more of a say about whom they married and when. These new expectations caused many conflicts between city parents and their older children.

Religion

Spain introduced Catholicism to Puerto Rico in 1511, organizing the island's population into religious communities or towns called *pueblos* that were presided over by Spanish Catholic bishops. The church and church plaza were the most important parts of the pueblo, the place where the townspeople socialized and the place where they celebrated religious occasions. Being Catholic (*católico*) did not just mean going to mass and taking sacraments; it meant being an active part of a Catholic community. Most rural peasants had both a deep faith and a deep sense of community, but worship for them was a highly individual and personalized act. Saints were looked on as personal *compadres,* or close friends, who could grant them favors in times of need. They prayed to the saints, lit candles to them, carried statues or images of them in religious processions, and built shrines to them in their homes. Every town celebrated fiestas in honor of its own patron saint.

The transfer of Puerto Rico to the United States in 1898 created a new and different role for organized religion. Most forms of Catholicism on the mainland did not include as personal a relationship with saints and did not provide the same sense of community. On the mainland, belonging to a church usually meant praying together and worshiping God in a prescribed way; it did not mean public demonstrations of faith such as holiday religious processions or fiestas. Nor did it mean providing emotional and often even financial support to other parishioners. Catholics from the mainland sent priests and set up expensive Catholic parochial schools that only the rich could afford. Mainland Protestants sent missionaries to convert islanders to Pentecostal, Evangelical, and Adventist sects. Protestants made converts (especially among the poor in large cities), but the country remained 80 percent Catholic. The mainland version of Catholicism caught on more in the cities than in the country, too.

Another form of traditional faith that persisted in some areas after the United States arrived on the island was spiritualism, the belief that the visible world is surrounded by an invisible world populated by spirits (both good and bad) who can break through to the visible world and attach themselves to human beings and change the course of human events. Many of the beliefs and superstitions are rooted in ancient Taino and African practices handed down from generation to generation. One aspect of this spiritualism is medicinal. Spiritualists believed that they could cure any naturally caused human illness with herbs and incantations. What the spiritualists could not cure, witches could. People believed that illness and misfortune were often the result of witchcraft (*brujería*) and could only be cured or lifted by the application of counter witchcraft. Every community had people (usually women) who held séances, claiming to be mediums with the ability to converse with the dead and with spirits in the invisible world.

Belief in spiritualism often went hand-in-hand with devout Catholicism, although the two belief systems might seem to be contradictory. Rather than decrease in popularity after the United States took over, spiritualism grew even stronger in some areas. People were overwhelmed with the changes in their family and community life and felt powerless to deal with the economic upheaval. So they turned to spiritualism in hopes of having some control over their life and environment.

Churches like this one in the village of Las Cayagus were often the center of a town's community as well as spiritual life.

For Puerto Ricans arriving in New York in the 1950s and 1960s, neighborhood stores and fruit stands stocked with familiar fruits, spices, and other traditional Puerto Rican foods provided a welcome touch of home in a strange and often overwhelming city.

CHAPTER TWO

LIFE IN A NEW LAND
A DIFFERENT KIND OF IMMIGRANT

It was a hot and humid summer night in the New York City *barrio*. While his parents and older sisters finished unpacking and settled into their fifth-floor walk-up, Roberto López decided to explore his new neighborhood. The old, tall apartment buildings were built so close together that they were almost on top of each other, a little overwhelming when you are used to a small town of spread-out, single-story wood and concrete houses. It stinks here, too, Roberto thought, like garbage and dogs and wet, burned wood. A lot of people were sitting outside on their stoops, and Roberto felt self-conscious walking down the sidewalk by himself. But they paid no attention to him; they were too busy talking and laughing or listening to the salsa music blaring out of their boom boxes. It seemed like everyone was out, young and old. Mothers pushing strollers stopped to chat with each other, while a couple of kids his age skillfully dodged parked and moving cars on their skateboards. Roberto decided they did not look that scary after all.

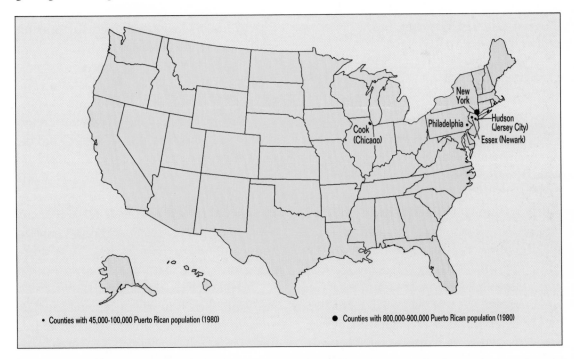

• Counties with 45,000-100,000 Puerto Rican population (1980)   ● Counties with 800,000-900,000 Puerto Rican population (1980)

While Puerto Rican communities can be found in major cities throughout the mainland United States, the heaviest concentrations are in the urban Northeast, especially in and around New York City. Puerto Ricans frequently travel back and forth between the island and the mainland for personal and business reasons.

Further down the street, an old woman was leaning out of an open window, yelling to her grandchildren that supper was ready, and when Roberto passed her house, he smelled the familiar and delicious rice and bean dish she had been cooking. When he got to the corner, he found several old men playing dominoes in front of the *bodega* (grocery store) on a folding table that looked every bit as rickety as they did. They laughed and drank beer, while some teenagers with expensive sneakers and stylish haircuts stopped for a moment to watch them before they headed off to their Friday night dance. Roberto stepped into the small, cluttered bodega and was delighted to find the *plátanos* (plantains) and *pasteles* he had been afraid he was going to have to live without. The bodega owner smiled at him from behind the counter. Maybe this New York was not going to be so bad after all.

Puerto Ricans Migrate to the Mainland

The first substantial wave of Puerto Ricans moving to the mainland began during World War I (1914-1918), when the booming U.S. war economy started producing unskilled jobs. Even more Puerto Ricans arrived during the prosperous roaring twenties, and by 1930, there were over fifty-three thousand living on the mainland. But immigration stopped again in the 1930s during the Great Depression, when jobs became just as scarce on the mainland as in Puerto Rico. But the U.S. economy improved substantially when the country entered World War II in 1941 and jobs were again plentiful. Because of German submarines patrolling the Atlantic waters off the East Coast, however, civilian passenger service between Puerto Rico and the States was suspended, and Puerto Ricans were unable to migrate to the mainland for the entire time of the war.

The second major migration wave began in the years immediately after the end of World War II (1945), when the mainland started experiencing severe shortages of farm labor. Not only was boat transportation again available, Puerto Ricans could now travel quickly and cheaply to mainland cities by plane. The U.S. government started a contract labor program that employed twenty thousand workers annually throughout the Northeast, in an area that extended as far west as Michigan.

Between 1950 and 1956, the U.S. economy experienced a tremendous postwar industrial boom. Factory jobs became available that paid ten times and more the wages Puerto Ricans were making on the island's sugar plantations. During that same period, Congress passed the McCarran Immigration Act, which made it difficult for people to immigrate to the United States from countries in war-torn Europe and Asia. As a result, newly arriving Puerto Ricans had access to many jobs for which they might otherwise have had to compete with other immigrant groups.

A number of economic factors in Puerto Rico also contributed to the large postwar migration to the mainland. The most important was the scarcity of jobs. Not only did the sugar plantations with their absentee mainland owners monopolize Puerto Rico's available farmland, they only offered work on a seasonal basis. Many of the tenant-farmer *jíbaros* were forced to move to Puerto Rico's cities to find work, only to find that work was scarce there, too.

In spite of large-scale industrial growth on the island, there were still not enough city factories to supply the number of jobs needed. And to make job competition even more fierce, Puerto Rico's population was booming at an alarming rate. At the same time, the cost of living was skyrocketing because the island now

THE MIGRANT FARM WORKERS

Not all Puerto Ricans moved to mainland cities. A large percentage of *jíbaros* needed work so badly that they were willing to travel back and forth from Puerto Rico to work as contract farm laborers. Harvesting sugar cane only provided work on the island from January to about the end of June, which meant that thousands of farm workers were available during the Northeast mainland's harvest season in autumn. When Puerto Rican laborers first arrived in the mid-1940s, there were no laws regulating their working conditions, and as a result, they were harshly exploited. They worked long hours for extremely low pay, and the housing conditions were terrible. If they complained, they were fired, often without getting paid what they had already earned. Newspapers in both the United States and Puerto Rico ran stories about the labor abuses and brought the issue to the attention of the U.S. Congress. In 1947, two laws were passed requiring mainland farmers who hired Puerto Rican laborers to provide contracts approved by the Puerto Rican Department of Labor. These contracts stipulated a maximum number of hours that could be worked in a given month and a minimum wage that had to be paid. The contracts also had provisions for housing, food, medical care, insurance, and transportation to and from the island. While the contracts did not solve all the difficulties Puerto Rican farm workers faced, it did end some of the abuses.

It is estimated that, even today, about twenty thousand Puerto Rican workers come to the mainland each year to harvest such crops as tobacco in Connecticut, fruits and vegetables in New York and New Jersey, and sugar beets in Michigan. Many of the workers have chosen to settle permanently in communities throughout the harvesting area.

had to depend on the mainland for much of its food and manufactured goods. Logically, unemployed islanders started looking to the mainland for jobs.

It is difficult to determine how many people actually moved to the mainland in any given year because, as U.S. citizens, Puerto Ricans did not have to pass through the usual immigration intake points that process foreigners. Another reason is that large numbers of Puerto Ricans were always traveling in both directions. Take the year 1960, for example, when 666,756 people departed from Puerto Rico for the mainland, but 643,014 traveled in the other direction, from the mainland to Puerto Rico. One cannot simply say that the net number of 23,742 was the number who actually migrated to the mainland, because it is impossible to know how many of these people were traveling back and forth for business reasons, education, vacations, family visits, baptisms, funerals, and so on.

While large numbers of Puerto Ricans continue to travel in both directions, the 1990 census showed that about 2.7 million Puerto Ricans now live on the mainland, with the largest concentration in New York State.

A Different Kind of Immigration

In many ways, settling into their lives on the U.S. mainland was much easier for Puerto Ricans than for foreign immigrants (from Europe, for example, or Asia or Mexico). Because Puerto Ricans were U.S. citizens, they did not need passports, visas, or any other bureaucratic paperwork, and they had the legal

Life for Puerto Ricans growing up on the Lower East Side of New York in the 1970s was often just as hard and challenging as it had been for the Italians, Jews, and other ethnic groups that arrived in the city before them. Many Puerto Ricans called this area of New York *Loisaida*.

right to travel and work anywhere in United States. They were already familiar with U.S. politics, constitutional law, school systems, currency, even the U.S. system of weights and measures. They were also the first immigrant group to have the benefit of airplane travel, which made the trip from island to mainland short and relatively cheap.

But at the same time, moving to the U.S. mainland was also much more difficult for Puerto Ricans than for foreign immigrants. Puerto Ricans (and other new minorities who arrived after World War II) came at a time when many of the dilapidated slum tenements in New York and other large U.S. cities were being torn down and replaced by public housing. This meant that most Puerto Ricans missed out on an important advantage that Irish, German, Jewish, Italian, and even Asian immigrants who had arrived earlier enjoyed:

ethnic neighborhoods. Instead, city agencies randomly assigned many poor Puerto Rican families to integrated public housing locations all over the city. This is not to say that Puerto Rican neighborhoods did not exist. When public housing was not available, newcomers were often forced to move into the city's remaining rat-infested, decaying old tenement buildings, creating small Puerto Rican neighborhoods in East Harlem, the South Bronx, parts of Manhattan's Upper West and Lower East Sides, and a tenement area in mid-Manhattan called "Hell's Kitchen."

Another advantage earlier Asian and European immigrants had over Puerto Rican newcomers was job availability. Puerto Ricans arriving on the mainland after the boom of the mid-1950s came just when increased technology and automation were eliminating the unskilled jobs that earlier immigrant groups

GOING HOME

Because of closeness and the low cost of transportation, many Puerto Ricans repeatedly visit their homeland or send their children for prolonged stays with relatives who still live on the island. But many also choose to return for good.

Some families who prosper on the mainland may later move back to Puerto Rico to start a business. Many others return because they are disillusioned with New York City or because work is scarce and the cost of mainland living too high. Adjusting to New York's winter climate is also a big factor, especially for older Puerto Ricans.

But just because Puerto Ricans choose to move back to their homeland does not mean they cannot change their minds again at a later date; they do not give up their U.S. citizenship or status as Americans just because they return to Puerto Rico.

had counted on to get started in the United States. Puerto Ricans also arrived at a time when factory wages were beginning to decline.

Why Move to New York?

More Puerto Ricans chose New York City as their destination than any other place on the mainland. One reason, of course is its large existing Puerto Rican community. Another is language. New York has long had Spanish-language newspapers, television and radio stations, bilingual public officials, and stores operated by Spanish-speaking merchants. It is easy to find familiar Puerto Rican foods, and there is always a strong possibility of finding people from one's hometown in a New York club or association. In addition, New York has traditionally had a great need for semiskilled laborers in the hotel, tourist, and garment industries.

New York may seem attractive to Puerto Ricans for other reasons, too. U.S. movies and TV shown in Puerto Rico have portrayed the city as a center of opportunity — and a place where one could enjoy freedom from prejudice and discrimination. Unfortunately, these representations of the city are often more myth than reality.

The Hard Adjustment to Life in New York

Adjusting to life in New York was much different than adjusting to life in San Juan or any other large Puerto Rican city. When landless tenant-farmer jíbaros moved to the island's cities to find work, they were totally unused

THE QUESTION OF CITIZENSHIP

Puerto Ricans became U.S. citizens in 1917, and the Commonwealth of Puerto Rico was established in 1952. Puerto Ricans do not pay federal income taxes. Nor do they vote in U.S. presidential elections (although beginning in 1980, they voted in presidential primaries). The only representation they have in Congress is an elected resident commissioner who only has committee voting privileges. Puerto Ricans have different opinions as to whether the island should remain a commonwealth, achieve statehood, or become totally independent.

Their distinctive spiritual and cultural traditions helped Puerto Ricans make the transition to life in large, industrialized cities. Stores like this *botánica* in New York's Spanish Harlem provided religious candles, statues of saints, and other familiar religious icons.

mals to defray the cost of food. After working in the city for a while and being exposed to schools and other urban institutions, shantytown families could gradually adapt to a more urban lifestyle.

In New York, however, people were immediately thrown into a whole new world with a different language, a different culture — even a different climate — with little time to learn and adapt. Here they were often ridiculed or criticized for their traditional ways, including how they raised their children and the outdated attitudes they had toward women. Without the support of ethnic neighborhoods, most *Nuyoricans* (as many Puerto Ricans living in New York City have chosen to call themselves) found the transition to life in New York sudden and painful.

On the mainland, even more than on the island, city life was especially hard on family relationships. Conflicts arose between husbands and wives when many Puerto Rican women looked for jobs to help support their families. Conflicts also arose when children came home from school and started to question their parents' authority and values. Relationships with extended family members and even godparents grew weaker because they generally lived so far away.

Puerto Ricans who opened small businesses

to city life. But because they were so desperately poor, most had to live in shantytowns, and horrible as the shantytowns were, at least they allowed people to preserve many of their familiar traditions while they made the transition to modern city life. People did not have to pay rent or utilities to live in shanties, and many kept chickens or other small farm aniin New York struggled, too. Competition with large, well-established stores made it hard to succeed, especially in high-crime neighborhoods where it was almost impossible to get insurance or adequate police protection. Many shopkeepers were forced out of business by urban renewal projects that did not adequately reimburse them for their loss. Puerto Ricans who were not fluent in English often ended up going out of business because they misinterpreted government laws and regulations or were swindled with deliberately confusing contracts.

Language was also a serious problem for Puerto Rican students. As recently as the 1970s and 1980s, up to 75 percent of Puerto Rican students dropped out before they graduated high school; of those who remained in school, over two-thirds were more than two years behind in reading skills. It was only when Puerto Rican political groups were successful in their push for bilingual education that these figures began to change.

In spite of the obstacles of poverty, illiteracy, and discrimination, and the weakening of families, Puerto Ricans have survived and even flourished. And as we will see in subsequent chapters, their strong family values, spiritual faith, and rich artistic expression continue to enrich mainstream U.S. culture.

In the 1960s, the U.S. Labor Department sponsored special programs such as this "mobile language classroom" to help New York Puerto Ricans learn English.

Traditional family roles are changing. Modern Puerto Rican fathers in Chicago and other large mainland cities are far more involved in raising their children than their own fathers and grandfathers had been.

CHAPTER THREE

FAMILY AND COMMUNITY
HANGING TOGETHER WITH CHANGE

Alma would much rather have spent New Year's Eve alone in her room watching MTV, but Papi said forget it. It was a night for family, and she had to be part of it. The house was already full of relatives, and the noise and confusion were overwhelming. Most of the younger cousins were playing Lotto and Monopoly in the rec room, but that was kid stuff and boring, so she thought she'd hang around upstairs for a while. Her uncles were already hotly debating a domino game on the card table in the corner, while their wives watched and made comments. (Alma could not remember a family party when the men were *not* clacking those ivory pieces around.) Mami was busy in the kitchen, filling the house with the most tantalizing smells of spicy meat *pasteles* and coconut-cinnamon pudding. Papi and the rest of the men were sitting around talking and drinking rum until the women were ready to serve dinner. Alma cringed when someone put on a CD and singer Felipe Rodríguez started wailing one of his endless melancholy ballads about faithless women and brokenhearted men.

In the other room, Alma's cousin Helena was sitting on the sofa with her brother José's fiancé, Maria, who had just moved from the island with her parents. Alma smiled at the incredible contrast between the two girls. Although they were both the same age — seventeen — Helena looked years older and much more sophisticated in her red, fitted Liz Claiborne dress. Her shoulder-length brown hair

was streaked with blonde, and her carefully manicured nails were painted a deep red to match the dress. And as she talked, she took long, elegant puffs on her cigarette. The shy *novia* was pretty, too, but did not seem to know it yet. Her knee-length dress was not as fashionable as Helena's, and her long hair was pulled back in a simple ponytail. When Maria spoke to people, she never looked them straight in the eye; good Catholic girls were supposed to be humble and subservient.

Mami said Maria would make a great Puerto Rican-style wife if José did not wait too long before marrying her. Alma overheard Helena talking to Maria: "Not me. What am I supposed to do, wear a black mantilla on my head and go to mass every day? I'm an American woman and I do what I want. My life is going to be different. I have an Anglo boyfriend. He's older and has a car. My parents don't know it, but I sneak out of the house sometimes at night to be with him. I can't wait till I'm away at college next year so I don't have to hear them trying to tell me what to do all the time." Alma wondered how long it would take for the city to change Maria, too.

Family Always Comes First

The migration of Puerto Ricans to the mainland has been for the most part a family migration. People have either come as families or they come to start their families in mainland cities, hoping to find more jobs and a higher standard of living than they could find

A New York Puerto Rican woman celebrates her birthday with her husband and young son. Whether someone turns 3, 33, or 103, birthdays in Puerto Rican families are always festive occasions.

in Puerto Rico. Puerto Ricans have traditionally emphasized the importance of family as a primary source of strength and support, especially during the process of migration. Even temporary Puerto Rican farm workers who traveled alone to the mainland for seasonal harvest work did so to support their families back home. Whatever their particular situation, Puerto Rican families have been profoundly affected by migration to the mainland in a number of ways.

The first change is in the marriage relationship itself. It was not uncommon among Puerto Rican islanders (especially the poor) for a man and woman to be joined in a consensual union, that is, to live together without the benefit of either a religious or a civil marriage ceremony. Although some consensual relationships continued to exist on the mainland, most Puerto Rican mainland couples found

that to be eligible for some valuable economic benefits (like widows' pensions, social security, and in many places admittance to public housing), they needed a marriage license. Many chose marriage simply because consensual unions were traditionally associated with the poor and they were working hard to rise to the middle class.

Another significant change has been the narrowing of family circles. Traditionally, Puerto Rican parents have been able to rely on the emotional and financial support of extended families who lived in the same neighborhood — or at least within traveling distance on the same island. The extended family is more than just grandparents, aunts, uncles, and first cousins; it includes in-laws, godparents, and distant cousins as well. Only couples who moved with their children into the Puerto Rican neighborhoods of New York and other

THE VALUE OF AN INDIVIDUAL, PUERTO RICAN STYLE

Both U.S. and traditional Puerto Rican cultures value individualism — the importance of the individual — but there is a significant difference in how the two cultures define the term. In the United States, a person is valued for his or her ability to compete for higher social status and material goods. In traditional Puerto Rican culture, on the other hand, it is the inner qualities of character that make a person unique and respected. Someone may be desperately poor, but if that person does her best to live within her circumstances with dignity and shows respect for other human beings, regardless of their social or economic standing, then she is considered a good, respected, and valued person.

The same is true if a person is incredibly wealthy: It is not the money that makes him valuable but the dignity of his lifestyle and his attitude toward other people. As a result, Puerto Ricans have been more apt to trust other people (as opposed to trusting government agencies or social institutions) — and also more apt to be hurt by another person's insults, rude behavior, or ruthless ambition.

---

large cities were able to live close to friends and other family members. The majority, who were scattered in public housing projects throughout the city, were often cut off from that support.

While Puerto Rican families today are much smaller, it was not unusual for first-generation migrant families to arrive on the mainland with eight or ten children. Without other relatives nearby to help, women who had to take care of large families were often overwhelmed with work and found it hard to cope. In addition, getting together with extended family members was also traditionally a woman's only acceptable opportunity to socialize. Those who who neither spoke English nor lived in Puerto Rican neighborhoods on the mainland felt particularly isolated.

Changing Roles of Men and Women

Another major impact of migration on Puerto Rican families has been the change in each person's role within the family and the friction those changes continue to cause. From the time of the Spanish conquest, much of Puerto Rican society has been based on the concept of *machismo* — the dominance of males. Traditionally, the husband/father was the most important and powerful member of the household, and the women (his wife and daughters), although revered and respected, were considered secondary. The male was traditionally the breadwinner and the protector of his family, while women were brought up to serve their husbands, raise devout children, and keep a spotless house. Despite her outwardly subservient role, however, the traditional Puerto Rican wife and mother was the one who disciplined the children and made most of the important family decisions, such as those regarding finances.

Women did not participate in public social affairs, but men could come and go as they pleased and spent a great deal of time socializing. Although women were encouraged to delay marriage until they had finished their education, they were not allowed to work outside of the house (unless they became nuns or teachers).

LUISA CAPETILLO: A POWERFUL ROLE MODEL

Luisa Capetillo may have been born into the island's privileged upper class, but she dedicated her life to improving the lives of the Hispanic workers — especially women — who were living on the mainland.

Capetillo arrived in New York in 1912, well educated and already politically active with socialist ideals and a dedication to helping the working class. In addition to working as a labor organizer and writing for numerous union and labor publications, Capetillo was years ahead of her time as an outspoken feminist, claiming that marriage was oppressive to women and that they needed to be financially independent.

In her book *Influencias de las ideas modernas (The Influence of Modern Ideas)*, Capetillo criticized machismo and its unfair double standard that demanded that brides had to be virgins while grooms did not; that wives had to be faithful when their husbands did not; and, whether they had to work outside the home or not, that wives were always held responsible for the upkeep of the home, keeping the marriage together, and raising the children. She urged women whose marriages did not give them equality and respect to get a divorce, especially those in physically abusive relationships. Capetillo opposed the oppression of marriage so intensely that she chose not to marry the man who fathered her four children. She also chose to remain politically active, working hard all her life at writing and labor organizing. She also continued to support the labor cause by reading to cigar workers in tobacco factories and by providing room and board for migrant lodgers.

Most men found that their wives' attitudes quickly changed when they moved to the mainland. Because the cost of living in the city was high and one income was often not enough to support a large family, women began to work outside the home. They could often find fac-

Puerto Rican women today are no longer restricted to raising children and managing a home. More and more highly qualified Puerto Rican women are breaking into corporate management or professions in law, medicine, science, or education.

COLOR: SUDDENLY IT'S A PUERTO RICAN "PROBLEM"

Puerto Ricans who moved to New York (and other areas) were angry and confused about the importance many mainland Americans placed on color to define a person's worth. Social and cultural interaction between races (including extensive intermarriage) had long been accepted in Puerto Rico. *Everyone* had a strong sense of dignity and identity, whether they were rich or poor, Black or white. Families of every background gathered together in town plazas to celebrate fiestas, form religious processions, and socialize with each other. It was not at all unusual for a child to have godparents of a different color. On the island, people were segregated by economic class, but if someone was able to advance economically through education or achievement, he or she was accepted in the higher class, regardless of color. Color did not define a Puerto Rican person's worth.

tory work more easily than men and when men found even low paying jobs scarce or temporary, women often became the family's main or even sole breadwinner.

While there are some Puerto Rican families who still maintain traditional family roles based on male superiority and dominance, most are changing, putting women on a more level ground with men. For many men, the change has been difficult and confusing. As women's self-esteem began to rise, men found themselves with less and less authority. Because men had been raised to define their own self-esteem in terms of their role as the family's protector and provider, they often found the fact that their wives worked humiliating. And when women who worked outside the home no longer had time for all the chores involved in raising children and running a household and began asking their husbands to help out, their requests frequently led to heated arguments.

As families adjust to the role changes, new generations of men are enjoying the greater involvement in raising their children and are as supportive of their wives' career achievements as their wives are of

COMPADRAZGO

One of the greatest honors that can be bestowed on a Puerto Rican is to be asked to be a child's godparent or *compadre*. It means much more than promising to raise the child if something should happen to its parents: It means playing an important role in the child's life, second only to being the child's parent. In earlier times, jíbaros would often ask someone with more wealth and social prestige than their own to be a godparent, like the landowners they worked for. Today, the godparents of the oldest child are usually the couple who were the maid of honor and best man at the child's parents' wedding. Friends of the family or brothers and sisters of the child's parents are also often chosen as godparents. Compadres are there for baptisms, birthdays, confirmations, communions, graduations, holidays, weddings — all the important events in a person's life. And whenever they come to visit, they bring gifts. In return, the godparents receive the child's total respect and devotion. Being asked to be a compadre is an honor that cannot be refused without offending the child's parents.

Unlike traditional nineteenth-century island schools where boys and girls were taught in separate class-rooms, Puerto Rican children today attend coed public schools. Many schools in large mainland cities help young new arrivals who only speak Spanish by offering bilingual classes.

theirs. Puerto Rican women are beginning to take advantage of educational opportunities for professional careers that their mothers and grandmothers were denied.

Growing Up on the Mainland

The role of children in Puerto Rican families is also changing. In traditional Puerto Rican families, children were dominated and protected by their parents. They had no rights and no say in any family affairs, and they were not allowed to participate in adult conversations. Their father's authority over them was absolute and was usually enforced by spanking or other mild corporal punishment. That did not mean, however, that children were unloved. Nor were they neglected. On the contrary.

Babysitting was a concept traditional Puerto Rican women did not believe in: A responsible mother did not leave her children with any stranger. To many Puerto Ricans, children are not considered intrusive, so there is never any need to leave them at home. They simply go wherever their mothers go. If that is not possible, then another relative cares for the child. In fact, Puerto Ricans feel they have a moral obligation to care for all of the children in their extended family, not just their own sons and daughters.

From the time they were born, parents and other relatives taught the young boys in the family to behave in a manly way and encouraged fistfights and other acts of *machismo*. Young girls, on the other hand, were closely guarded by their parents and older siblings. They were expected to be submissive and obedient and to behave like "good girls" — for most Puerto Ricans, that meant good Catholic girls — at all times. Girls were separated from boys in classrooms and most social functions. They were not allowed to socialize with more than one boy before getting married, and all their dates had to be chaperoned.

The status of children changed drastically when families arrived on the mainland. First of all, children were regarded as people with certain rights, such as the right to a free public education. While this gave all parents, rich and poor alike, the opportunity to educate their children, at the same time parents were afraid and resentful because they lost a certain amount of their control. Boys and girls could not be kept socially separated if they were taught in coeducational classes and attended school social functions together. As children (especially girls) became more independent and able to make decisions for themselves, they began to question parental authority, which became another source of family tension.

Courtship and Marriage

In older generations, a girl was restricted to the house of her parents until she got married and was then restricted to the house of her husband. While most contemporary mainland Puerto Ricans socialize, date, become

A group of teens on their way to a sweet-sixteen party in rented vintage cars and formal wear. In earlier days, a Puerto Rican girl could not socialize with a boy unless a chaperon was present and the boy planned to marry her. Today, most Puerto Rican teens join in all typical mainland dating customs.

While teenage pregnancies have become a growing problem in the United States, often trapping young mothers in a life of poverty, teens like this young Puerto Rican mom are being encouraged to finish high school and even college to ensure the best chance for themselves and their children.

engaged, and get married in ways that are similar to those of their non-Puerto Rican neighbors, U.S. dating and courtship practices still seem too permissive to many of the more traditional and conservative Puerto Rican parents.

Puerto Rican girls today enjoy being with other people their own age, both boys and girls. They expect to go out on dates with a number of different boys — without a chaperone— and consider it natural to associate with boys at school and in their neighborhoods. Some want to get married early, while others prefer to put off marriage until they are well out of college and established in a professional career. In either case, the concept of *machismo* is no longer acceptable in their social relationships. Boys are having to learn to accept them as equals.

To a more traditional-minded father, this kind of behavior may seem scandalous and reflect badly on the rest of the family. Like his father and grandfather before him, he would expect his daughters to pursue a higher education (or at least finish high school) before

she gets married, then focus her life on marriage, children, and the management of her husband's household. The purpose of her education would not be to pursue a career but to have it to fall back on if the marriage does not work out or something happens to her husband. Unchaperoned dating, dropping out of school, and teenage pregnancy are simply not options, in a father's eyes, for a traditionally raised, devout Catholic daughter.

Unfortunately, dropping out of school and becoming pregnant have become a reality for many mainland Puerto Rican girls, particularly in larger cities. Like those within the U.S. culture at large, Puerto Rican teens on the mainland enjoy much more dating freedom. One of the effects of this liberation is that girls are less likely to pursue a higher education (many do not even finish high school) because they quit to get a job or to get married. Another negative effect of changing times has been a rising rate of teenage pregnancies.

Boys, on the other hand, always had much more freedom when it came to traditional dating practices. They were encouraged to prove their *machismo* or masculinity by freely dating as many different girls as possible. The more experienced they became, the better. At the same time, however, they were expected to only propose to and marry *novias* — that is, "good," conservatively raised girls who were chaste, devoutly religious, and still under the protection of their fathers and older brothers. In conservative, traditional families on the mainland this double-standard is still strongly reinforced. A boy's relationship with the girl he intends to marry has to be formal and correct. Ideally, this means regular visits to the girl's home in the company of her family, chaperoned dates, and the formal request to the father for her hand in marriage.

Traditionally, for couples who choose to be married in the Catholic Church, it was the bride's family who was responsible for almost all of the costs involved. Today, many Puerto Ricans belong to Protestant religious sects that do not insist that a wedding include flowers, a formal wedding dress, and an expensive reception. The same is true of civil marriage ceremonies.

Growing Old

Puerto Rican families have traditionally held their older members in high esteem, according them the same obedience and respect they show their parents. When several generations of an extended family live under the same roof (or at least nearby), the grandparents often take care of the younger children and offer other kinds of support.

Traditionally, death is seen not as an end but as a new beginning. Nevertheless, out of

ANTOJOS (CRAVINGS)

The first pregnancy of a young married Puerto Rican woman is a joyous occasion, and she is traditionally pampered by family members, especially her mother-in-law and her husband. In many traditional families, pregnancy was the one occasion of a woman's life when she was allowed and even encouraged to indulge herself. It was totally acceptable for her to appeal to the sympathy and guilt of those around her to get them to help satisfy her *antojos,* or cravings. Most had to do with food (like waking her husband in the middle of the night to demand that he go out and buy her pickled plantains and some coconut ice cream or some other hard-to-find and weird food combination). Everyone traditionally gave in to a pregnant woman's antojos because it was believed that to do otherwise would create undue anxiety and harm to both mother and unborn child. Some people went so far in believing this superstition that they actually felt an unfilled antojo could even result in a miscarriage.

love and respect for the person who died and for the benefit of his or her soul, the closest members of the family are expected to wear dark clothes and abstain from dancing and other such festivities for an extended period of time to mourn their loss. In more traditional families, widows, orphans, mothers, or other relatives sometimes vow to wear black or not cut their hair for the rest of their lives. These vows are called *promesas*, from the Spanish word for promise.

The *Nuyorican* Community

In many ways, community ties are just as important as family ties. Although a large percentage of Puerto Ricans who settled in New York first lived in public housing throughout the city, New York did develop a good-sized

Despite difficult living conditions, Puerto Rican communities like New York's Spanish Harlem are far from dismal and depressing. Alive with Spanish shop signs, the pounding beat of salsa music, and the spicy tastes and smells of traditional Puerto Rican cooking, Puerto Rican neighborhoods are a delight to the senses.

Puerto Rican community along East 116th Street. In the 1930s, this area came to be known as *El Barrio* (the Neighborhood) and as Spanish Harlem. Today, this area is still a thriving Puerto Rican neighborhood, and the many small, family-run businesses like the *bodegas* (corner grocery stores), cafés, and restaurants give the area a distinctly Puerto Rican flavor. Public notices and the advertisements plastered on the neighborhood's billboards, subway cars, and buses are all in either Spanish or both English and Spanish, and local newsstands carry the popular daily Spanish newspaper *El Diario-La Prensa,* which is staffed mainly by Puerto Ricans. Area radio stations play salsa and Latin hip-hop, and TV stations broadcast a wide variety of Spanish-language programs, from educational and news shows

to variety shows, *novelas* (soap operas), cartoons, and Latin MTV.

Other Puerto Rican Communities

Of course, not every Puerto Rican on the mainland lives in New York City, and most large U.S. cities have Spanish-language media, both local and national, including newspapers, magazines, television, and radio, all of which cater not only to Puerto Ricans but to local Mexican, Caribbean, and Central American communities as well. There were sizable Puerto Rican communities in cities like Boston, Chicago, Miami, and New Orleans as early as 1920. While Puerto Ricans have settled in every U.S. state, today over 90 percent of them are concentrated in the larger cities of just eight states: New York, New Jersey, Illinois, Florida,

California, Pennsylvania, Connecticut, and Massachusetts. The Puerto Rican community in Chicago is the second largest on the mainland, although it did not really start to grow until after World War II.

The Hard Fight Continues

The problems Puerto Rican newcomers faced when they arrived in New York and other mainland cities were tremendous — but Puerto Ricans refused to be overwhelmed. Instead, they fought back. Where they could not live in close, ethnic neighborhoods, they created their own substitute communities by organizing hundreds of communal associations. They sponsored clubs to help newcomers, formed bilingual educational programs to improve their children's educational opportunities, and created civic, educational, religious, business, labor, and social groups to promote the rights of Puerto Ricans, not just in New York but throughout the country. They organized housing clinics to inform Puerto Rican tenants of

their rights and worked to increase the number of Puerto Rican police officers, firefighters, and teachers. They formed a number of cultural groups such as ASPIRA and the South Bronx Bi-Lingual Performing Arts Center that work to help young Puerto Rican people become aware of their cultural heritage. Puerto Ricans have also become politically active in every arena from neighborhood politics to the U.S. Congress.

Businesspeople have fought back, too. Over two thousand Puerto Rican merchants joined together and created the Spanish Merchants Association to fight for programs to help Puerto Rican businesspeople make it in New York City. Laborers started fighting for their rights by joining or organizing unions (especially in the garment and hotel service industries). In addition to these sources of support in the Puerto Rican community, one of the most powerful strengths Puerto Ricans have always drawn on to fight adversity and maintain their culture is their deep spiritual faith.

Puerto Rican communities in Chicago and other large mainland cities have always thrived because they act as an extended family, providing each member with financial, emotional, and cultural support.

Children dress up to march in New York's annual Dia de los Reyes (Three Kings Day) Parade, just one of the many public religious processions Puerto Ricans stage to celebrate their rich spiritual traditions.

RELIGION AND CELEBRATIONS
CELEBRATE LIFE, CELEBRATE FAITH

Luis Colón fidgeted as his mother knotted his tie. The black suit was already starting to itch — he hoped the priests would get it over with fast so he could beat it back home in a hurry and change into normal human jeans and sneakers. Luis sighed as his younger brother stared at him in awe. Maybe it was worth it. After all, First Holy Communion meant that from now on, no one would treat him like a baby anymore. And besides, there'd be twenty other kids there going through the same ordeal.

As his mom tied the oversized red ribbon around his elbow, she quizzed him on catechism questions, even though she knew how hard he had studied these last few months and how well he knew the answers. If Luis was nervous about meeting with Father Nuñez, it was more about his first confession than about the examination. What if he forgot to confess something, something important? He would tell the Father about the times he yelled at his parents and the time he and some friends stole strawberries from a neighbor's garden, but could not think of anything else to confess. But being unaware of your sins was no excuse. The nuns knew a lot better than you did what was a sin and what was not; they'd had technical training in those things, and they did not miss a thing.

How many times had one of his nun teachers rapped his knuckles with a metal ruler for sins he had absolutely no idea he had committed? Like daydreaming in class or laughing at something serious someone had said. Was he really expected to wear this suit all morning through church and then all afternoon at the party, too?

When his mother finally stopped fussing over his appearance, Luis went looking for his best friend, Eddie, and found him out on the porch with his dad, Eddie's parents, and his Aunt Carmencita. The house was already filled with guests: aunts, uncles, cousins, grandparents, godparents, neighbors, and friends. They had come to see their Luis receive the host for the first time; nothing would have kept them home. His godparents had flown all the way up from San Juan. Eddie's family was Protestant, and Luis had to explain to them what Holy Communion was all about. From now on, he was responsible for everything he did, and if he did something bad, God would punish him for his sins. The only way to set things right again in God's eyes was to confess them to a priest and ask for forgiveness. Eddie said he was glad his church did not have confession; it made God sound so scary.

As they were getting ready to leave, Aunt Carmencita pulled Luis aside and, as she gave him a quick hug, pressed a small silver charm into his palm and murmured some strange-sounding magical words in blessing. Holy Communion was fine, Carmencita knew, but just to make sure her favorite nephew would be protected from evil spirits, she gave him the image of *Chango*, the important *Santería* deity also known as Santa Barbara.

Puerto Rican women of all ages are enthusiastic participants in the church choir of the First Congregational Church of Chicago. While the vast majority of Puerto Ricans belong to the Roman Catholic Church, there is a minority who belong to various Protestant denominations.

Forming a Unique
Spiritual Tradition

The majority (about 80 percent) of Puerto Rican people consider themselves Catholic, although some do not regularly attend mass and prefer to practice their faith at home. Most of the rest are members of such Protestant sects as the Baptists, Methodists, Lutherans, Episcopalians, and Pentecostals.

Puerto Rican Catholicism is strikingly different from the Catholicism practiced anywhere else in the world, mainly because of the island's history. The Spanish may have tried to convert the islanders, who they thought were pagans, to their European religion, but in the end, the highly evolved spirituality of the Taino and African cultures did not embrace Catholicism so much as simply incorporate it into their existing belief systems, changing symbols here and there to please the Spanish. As a result, for Catholic Puerto Ricans, religion has always meant more than believing in God, participating in the Mass, and holding strictly to Church doctrine; it has also meant a deep abiding faith in the powers of the Virgin Mary and the saints, which are not only regarded as holy figures but as friends and *compadres*. In addition to hanging and wearing crucifixes, believers hang pictures and place statuettes of the Virgin and the saints in their homes, cars, and work places, and they build shrines, light candles, wear medals, pray, and make vows to them. In return for such devotion, they hope to receive favors and protection against harm.

Puerto Rican Catholicism has also traditionally meant a loyalty to family and community traditions and public as well as private displays of worship such as fiestas and processions.

One of the most important aspects of traditional Puerto Rican Catholicism is the celebration of rites of passage such as baptism, communion, confirmation, marriage, the anointing of the sick, last rites, and Christian burial. Each rite involves special ceremonies and the receiving of special sacraments. Each is necessary for a person to rise to heaven when he or she dies. Traditional Puerto Rican families continue to celebrate these rites today.

Rites of Passage

Baptism. The initiation into Christianity usually begins several weeks after a person is born, with the sacrament of baptism. This sacrament is administered by a priest in a special church ceremony in the presence of the parents and other special people, such as family members, the chosen compadres, and friends. Children are also given their Christian names when they are baptized.

First Holy Communion. The next important rite, the sacrament of First Holy Communion, takes place when a child is believed to have reached the "age of reason," usually the age of eight or nine, when he or she has become old enough to be held accountable before God and the community for his or her actions. Preparation for First Holy Communion includes studying the catechism or main points of the Catholic faith. Children are told that they are no longer innocent and that every transgression from that point on is punishable by God. They are also taught that through confession of their misdeeds, things can be set right again. To receive First Communion, the child is presented by his or her parents to the priest for examination and first confession.

Confirmation. In Puerto Rico, the next sacrament — confirmation — is commonly referred to as *obispar* because when Spain still ruled the island, it was one of the few occasions in a rural Catholic's life that he or she encountered a bishop (*obispo*). Originally, children were confirmed when they were quite young (usually sometime between baptism

JUST IN CASE

It used to be that babies born to rural peasants in Puerto Rico would be "unofficially" baptized as soon as they were born by the *comadrona* (midwife) who delivered them. The infant mortality rate on the island was so high that many babies died before they could receive official baptism from the village priest, and dying without receiving the sacrament meant the child could not go to heaven. Ideally, a church baptism was performed within the first few weeks of a child's life, but because of the security the midwife's *baptismo de auga* provided newborn children, parents often postponed the official baptism, sometimes for years, until the *compadres,* or godparents, they had chosen were able to afford the ceremony and the expected presents.

As a result, the midwife (called *comadrona* or *partera*) became a godmother to all the children in her village, if only a temporary one.

and First Communion), because, as with baptism, infant mortality was high and confirmation was another important sacrament that people should receive before they died. Today, most Puerto Rican Catholics are confirmed when they reach the age of about fifteen or sixteen. This important rite of passage acknowledges that the young person has reached maturity and is now ready to become an adult member of the church. Preparation for confirmation takes much time and commitment and includes increased church involvement, community service work, and weekend confirmation classes for about two years. A child often receives another set of godparents on this occasion.

Marriage. Marriage is one of the most joyous rites of celebration. The ceremony in the candle-lit church, however, is long and solemn, with special prayers interspersed with beautifully sung arias. Traditionally, it is the groom who is responsible for providing an offering to the priest and for paying whatever costs the church may require. For couples who choose a church marriage, it is the bride's family who is responsible for almost all of the other costs involved. This includes the formal, white bridal gown, a *desposorio* (a small celebration for the intimate family the day before the wedding), and the *bodas* (the big celebration on the day of the wedding).

The groom is expected to provide the bride with *las arras*, usually twenty silver pieces to symbolize his ability and willingness to support and provide for his future household. The bride's father provides the wedding feast with music and drink, but often everyone in the bride's extended family helps out with part of the cooking or other preparations.

In older times, everyone in town was invited to the celebration, mainly because everyone in town was somehow distantly related to either the bride or the groom. Even today, where extended family members may be scattered all over Puerto Rico and the mainland, there is still the expectation in traditional families that everyone in the family will attend. It is not unusual for both the bride's and groom's families to have their houses filled with visiting relatives who flew in to help celebrate.

Now, as before, baptisms and marriages are occasions for Puerto Ricans to visit with one another, to catch up on the latest news or gossip, and to renew old bonds.

Rites for the Ill and Dying. The Catholic Church also offers strength and sacrament for the ill and dying. Traditionally, when it became obvious that an ill person was beyond the help of either a physician or a *curandera* (herb healer), relatives would seek out the town *rezador*, a man or woman whose function it was to pray over the ill person and ask for divine intercession for his or her cure. If a cure was not still not possible, the rezador would pray for *la gracia de un buen morir* (resignation and a good death). At this point, the ill person, if conscious, might want to summon someone he or she wished to apologize to before dying or someone to ask for a special favor.

PERSONAL SHRINES

The practice of the shrine, or *hermita,* was often carried over to home altars and devotional tables where flowers, offerings, lighted candles, and statues in effect made part of the home a private chapel. When people were too poor to buy expensive statues of saints, they made their own out of local materials, thus giving rise to the art of the *santos,* or homemade religious figures.

When it became apparent that death would come very soon, the rezador would gather the person's family and friends around the deathbed to help him or her take leave of his temporal existence. They often remained at the bedside, maintaining a night-long *velada,* or vigil. Everyone prays during this time, including the dying person if he or she is still conscious, except for one person, who would go for the priest to administer the last rites, another sacrament necessary to absolve the dying of their sins and allow them to pass to heaven.

Traditionally, when a person dies, the corpse remains in the family home overnight, and during that time people are permitted to come and pay their respects. This is called *velar al muerto* or *velorio.* The family offers food and drink, and everyone sings special prayers for the dead. The next day, following burial services presided over by the priest and a final farewell given by a close friend or rela-

tive, the *dolientes,* or mourners, return home to comfort one another over a family meal. That evening and for the next seven days, family and friends meet again to pray for the repose of the soul, thus completing *la novena,* or nine days of prayer. An anniversary velorio is held on the same day each year in remembrance of the person's death.

A Cycle of Faith and Celebration

Christmastide and Holy Week. The three most important holidays for most Puerto Ricans fall between December 24 and January 6: Christmas Eve, New Year's Eve, and Three Kings, or Epiphany Day. The celebration actually starts more than a week before Christmas, however, with nine consecutive days of dawn masses called *misas de aguinaldo.* (*Aguinaldo* is also the word for Christmas hymn or carol.) Hymns are sung to the accompaniment of guitar, castanets, tambourines,

Not even a camel marching down Broadway can surprise most New Yorkers. This handsomely dressed specimen is part of the Puerto Rican community's annual Three Kings Day Parade.

Mainland Puerto Ricans often celebrate traditional feast days and other holidays in neighborhood community centers like this one in New York's Spanish Harlem.

and organ. After leaving the church, noisy groups of friends and relatives often stop at a bakery on the way home. The freshly baked bread, still hot from the oven, makes a delicious holiday breakfast.

Navidades, the celebration of Christmas, is a holiday traditionally reserved for family, especially on Christmas Eve. Throughout "*Noche Buene*" and the early hours of Christmas Day, groups of kinfolk and close neighbors go from house to house, where they are offered some rum or light refreshments (such as rice with coconut, papaya sweets, crullers, and other delectable treats) before they continue on to the next home. Some go to church to attend the *Misa de Callo* (Midnight Mass).

Traditionally, Puerto Ricans do not put up a Christmas tree or exchange gifts on Christmas Day but celebrate instead with a quiet day at home with the family. This is changing in many households because so many other American children are showered with gifts on Christmas and enjoy brightly decorated trees that young Puerto Rican children often feel left out. Instead of a tree, Puerto Ricans traditionally set up a colorfully decorated altar with hand-painted figures of the Three Wise Men and many lighted candles.

The Feast of the Epiphany, or Three Kings Day, celebrates the day the Three Wise Men arrived in Bethlehem to visit the newly born Baby Jesus and for this reason is the traditional day of gift giving. The night before, small children excitedly place freshly cut grass in boxes underneath their beds. That night, after they have fallen asleep, the Three Wise Kings, Caspar, Melchior, and Balthazar, stop on the way to Bethlehem to let their hungry horses eat the grass. In the morning, the children wake up to find that the kings have filled their boxes with gifts in gratitude. In the past, it was also customary to celebrate (with prayer and processions) the Octave of Bethlehem, the eight days following Epiphany.

Lent and Eastertide. Lent is a religious season observed for forty days, beginning with Ash Wednesday and ending with Easter Sunday. In commemoration of Christ's crucifixion and subsequent resurrection, it is a time for prayer, introspection, fasting, and sacrifice. Lent is more strictly observed on the island, where, during Holy Week, the week before Easter, everything closes down, including gov-

Even the youngest Puerto Rican Catholics dress up in their best clothes for early morning mass on Easter Sunday.

The period of Lent observed by Catholics before Easter is a somber and serious time. *Via Crucis*, a procession reenacting the journey of Jesus to the site of his crucifixion, is just one of many observances Puerto Rican Catholics participate in during Lent.

ernment offices. People spend a great deal of time in church praying and participating in solemn religious processions. Catholics are expected to make sacrifices during Lent, like avoiding meat and giving up amusements such as television. After a joyous mass on Easter Sunday, the whole family traditionally heads over to Grandma's for a special holiday dinner.

A Year-round Fiesta Cycle. In contrast to the solemn observance of Lent and Holy Easter Week, the patron saint festivals held year-round all over the island are a time for drinking, dancing, gambling, and just having fun. A major celebration not just on the island but in large mainland cities such as New York and Chicago is the Fiesta de San Juan, held on June 24. Fifty years ago, these fiestas had a much more religious tone; today, the music and dancing remain, but the religious aspect is no longer

that important. The parks are full of music and parades, Ferris wheels, merry-go-rounds (*caballitos*, meaning "little horses"), and penny-pitching booths, and it was customary to set off complex and beautiful fireworks in the evenings. There were troubadour competitions (where contestants had to improvise *décimas*, ten-line ballads), sack races, tricks with greased pigs, and many other games in which both young and old participated.

Each town holds an eight-day celebration for its own particular patron saint. With seventy-eight towns on the island holding such festivals, there is plenty of fun available all year-round.

All Souls' Day (November 2). On November 2, relatives who died during the previous year are remembered with flowers and burning candles at the grave site. In memory

These dancers celebrate the Fiesta Santiago Apostol, also known as Loiza Aldea, one of many regional island festivals that have moved to the mainland.

of other departed relatives, prayers are offered at home with candles burned in front of a photo of the deceased. Some choose to make a donation to the church to have their loved ones remembered in a special mass of the dead.

Protestantism

Protestantism was considered heresy when the Spanish ruled Puerto Rico. Not until the 1800s did the Spanish Crown permit a Protestant church to be built, and only then after Queen Victoria interceded on behalf of several English families who had settled there in Ponce and Vieques. After 1898, when Puerto Rico became a U.S. territory, Protestant groups in the United States looked southward to the Caribbean and saw over a million potential converts.

To avoid needless rivalry, these Methodists, Baptists, and Episcopalians agreed to divide up the new territory beforehand so that each would have its own exclusive region to seek converts. They did not make many converts, however, on the poverty-stricken island until rural Puerto Ricans started to break out of their poverty and create a middle class in the 1950s.

Today, only about one-quarter of all Puerto Rican Protestants belong to major sects; the rest belong to revivalist movements such as the Pentecostal and the Seventh Day Adventists, many of which demand strict adherence to rules of dress and behavior, including abstinence from tobacco, drugs, and alcohol.

There are few regular congregations in mainland cities that are run by and for Puerto Ricans, and so many neighborhoods start their own small "storefront" churches instead. Because a storefront church is small, informal, and intimate (with about sixty to eighty members at most), it is not as intimidating to new arrivals as a large, mostly non-Latino congregation might be.

In addition to spirituality and services in Spanish, storefront churches offer faith healing, as well as emotional and practical support to people new to an urban mainland environment. The ministers are also Puerto Rican and usually from the working class and therefore can identify strongly with their parishioners. Storefront churches are much less popular with second- and third-generation mainland Puerto Ricans, however.

THAT OLD-TIME RELIGION

You can hear them a block away — singing and clapping hands to the rhythm of electronic keyboard, tambourines, and drums. It sounds like that old-time religion, only the words are in Spanish. The church is a long, narrow storefront with a raised platform at one end on which a preacher stands holding onto a podium, waiting for the last stragglers to come in and take a seat. Behind him, a quartet of teenage musicians are playing Christian rock with a stirring Latin beat. When he thinks that no more people will come, the preacher starts the service by leading a Spanish hymn, then calling on congregation members to "testify" or confess their sins. A woman sings a moving Spanish song to the accompaniment of an acoustic guitar, and then the preacher reads Bible scripture and delivers his sermon. After another moving Spanish song, the preacher calls upon those who are ill or disabled to use their faith to heal themselves, to the enthusiastic cheers of the rest of the congregation. After the service, some of the parishioners go out for coffee.

Spiritism

Another facet of religious life that is still important to many Puerto Ricans is an interest in *Espiritismo*, or spiritism. This is a religious practice rooted in the belief that people in this world can establish contact with the spirit world and then use this power either to heal and protect or to cause illness, destruction, or even death. There are many different types of spiritistic folk religions, ranging from *Mesa Blanca* and *Santería* (both of which call on the power of the saints) to *Brujería* (the practice of witchcraft) and *Curandera* (herbal folk medicine). It is important to note that spiritism is not simply an alternative belief system. A person can be a devout Catholic and still seek out the magic powers of a *santero* (spiritual medium) or a *curandero* (folk healer).

In Mesa Blanca, a *presidente,* or medium, holds a group séance and through prayer and meditation summons the spirit of a recently departed soul who is believed to be causing problems for a certain person or persons. The presidente either tries to persuade the spirit to depart and leave its victims in peace (if it is basically a good spirit) or tries to exorcise it (if it is a malevolent one).

Santería also deals with spirit problems but in a different way. Santería incorporates African deities (*orichas*) into its spirit hierarchy as well as saints; its mediums (*santos*) pray to both for power to heal. In the process, the medium often becomes possessed by one or the other in the course of a séance.

Followers of both Santería and Mesa Blanca believe that a human being has both an animal (or physical) nature and a God-given spirit. In the case of most people, when the body dies, the spirit gradually abandons the earthly plane to rejoin the world of other incorporeal spirits, a process that usually takes nine days (the exact time the novena lasts after burial).

Spirits who have devoted their lives to material and sensual gratification, however, may take a lot longer and get stuck hovering a few inches above the earth as intranquil spirits who spend their time interfering with the lives of the living.

A spirit may stay on that plane if it still feels attached to its earthly belongings or has a special loving attachment to someone still living. Some have an unmet obligation, such as an unpaid debt or an important favor they still owe someone. People who died prematurely — especially through fatal accidents, suicide, or violent crime — can sometimes hover indefinitely on this plane. The only hope these spirits have of moving up the ranks of the spiritual hierarchy is for living humans to "give them light" by performing certain services on their behalf, such as reciting prayers, lighting candles, and offering flowers. If they are not "given light," these restless spirits could fall under the power of evil earthly sorcerers (called *brujos*) who use them to harm their enemies.

When they are given light, intranquil spirits rise to join the spirits of friends and relatives who have become free of earthly attraction but nevertheless watch over and protect their surviving loved ones. The next level up contains the spirits of great heroes and leaders (John Kennedy, for example, or Martin Luther King, Jr.), whose pictures and statues are often displayed on household altars. The rank after that holds the spirits of saints, and the one directly under God holds pure spirits such as warriors, angels, and *orichas* (certain African deities).

Brujería (witchcraft or black magic) can be practiced by mediums of either Santería or Mesa Blanca. Santería is often associated more with the Afro-Caribbean practice of voodoo and is therefore more predisposed to black magic. To perform sorcery, certain mediums are believed to have a special relationship with "dark spirits" whose evil help they can summon by making a charm that contains something belonging to the intended victim. The medium then buries it with an appropriate ritual in some outdoor place, causing the victim illness, accident, or other specified misfortune.

Curanderismo is the practice of folk medicine that uses spiritualism and magic as well as herbal remedies to cure illness. *Curanderos* treat everything from minor ailments to serious conditions like asthma, diabetes, and even cancer, but they are not limited just to treating physical problems. They are also often consulted to resolve marital conflicts, family or business disputes, or to cure depression. The basis of curanderismo is that all illness is caused by evil or misguided spirits.

Whether one believes in spiritism or not, Santería, Mesa Blanca, voodoo, brujería, and curanderismo are a fact of life not only in the Caribbean, but in mainland cities as well. Every city in the United States where there is a substantial Puerto Rican population has at least one *botánica*, a neighborhood boutique selling magical and spiritual paraphernalia. In New York, there are many.

Whatever potion, talisman, candle, or icon you believe will bring luck, jinx an enemy, bless a home, or attract a lover — it can be found at a neighborhood Puerto Rican *botánica*.

AS CLOSE AS YOUR CORNER BOTÁNICA

Originally, *botánicas* just sold mysterious-sounding medicinal herbs and plants like *yagrumo* and *anamu*. Over the years, they have come to sell much more, including a vast assortment of incense, candles, books on magic and healing, and statuary for practicing different types of spiritism. There are ready-made potions for removing jinxes, blessing houses, acquiring money, and winning love, with vivid names like *Arraza con todo* (Demolishes everything) and *Harás mi voluntad* (You will do as I say), not to mention the intriguing *Yo puedo y tu no* (I can and you cannot). If this assortment of items does not offer quite what you need, the proprietor usually has a number of items for the serious *santero* or *curandera* in the back room, including live lizards and toads, as well as the horns, hides, teeth, fangs, claws, and even excrement of more exotic animals.

Puerto Rico's rich and spicy cuisine is often created with exotic fruits, vegetables, and spices that can only be purchased on the mainland from Puerto Rican neighborhood vendors.

CHAPTER FIVE

Customs, Expressions, and Hospitaliy
Culture with Flair

Once upon a time, a little girl named Marisol lived with her mother in a small Puerto Rican town called Aguadilla. One day, Marisol was kidnapped by an ugly green-and-purple little man with curled-up toes who tied her up in his sack. His intention was to trick people into believing he had a magic singing sack and then to get rich on what he would charge them to hear it sing. So he told Marisol that whenever he said, *"¡Canta, saquito, canta!"* ("Sing, little sack, sing!"), she must sing a song — or else he would hit her with a stick. They traveled from town to town, and in every town square, the ugly little man commanded her to sing, and in every town, the people clapped their hands and cheered in amazement at his magic, singing sack. In payment, they gave the man plates of rice, fried chicken, and ripe mangos, but the greedy little man kept almost all of it for himself and gave only a few scraps to Marisol.

One day, they came back to the town of Aguadilla, where one of the many townspeople gathered in the square to hear the singing sack was Marisol's mother, who immediately recognized the singing. To rescue her daughter, she tricked the ugly little man by telling him she liked his performance so much that she wanted to cook him a chicken stew but needed a pot of water. He was so greedy that he dropped the sack, grabbed her pot, and ran down to the river. As soon as he was gone, the mother untied the bag and let Marisol escape. Then all the townspeople helped them fill the bag with rotten mangoes and old coconut shells. "Your singing is so wonderful," Marisol's mother said to the ugly little man when he returned, "Why don't you take it to show the king?"

The greedy little man forgot all about the chicken stew, hoisted the sack onto his shoulders, and ran right off to the king's palace. The king called the queen, his soldiers, and all of his servants to the throne room to hear the magic singing sack. *"¡Canta, saquito, canta!"* the ugly little man yelled several times, but the sack remained silent. Stamping his foot in rage, the little man took his stick and whacked the bag as hard as he could. Still the sack said nothing. When he whacked it again, the sack broke open and all the coconut shells and rotten mangoes burst out, splattering not just the king and queen but the very walls of the throne room and everyone else in it as well. The king was so furious that he ordered his soldiers to throw the little man into a cold, dark dungeon, where he would have only a stone floor to sleep on and meager scraps of food to eat. The ugly little man was never heard from again.

Stories like this one (*"¡Canta, Saquito!"* — "Sing, Little Sack!") are part of Puerto Rico's popular folk tradition — the stories and legends, songs, dances, games, holiday customs, superstitions, and modes of speaking that are

The famed Puerto Rican Traveling Theater often stages its performances at New York's Lincoln Center for the Arts.

FOLK STORIES AND LEGENDS

Some of the most most fascinating examples of indestructible Puerto Rican folklore can be found in the anonymous adventure stories of three beloved folk heroes: Juan Bobo, Juan Animala, and Juan Cuchilla. Although each is the hero of his own stories, they have a number of things in common. All are very poor peasants. All are constantly caught in jams or are the victims of terrible misfortunes, and all have to survive somehow by their wits.

Juan Bobo is a humble and serene man who takes the people he meets at face value and tries to solve his problems in a straightforward way. What makes him endearing is his innocence and his often exasperating (and humorous) lack of good sense. For example, in one story, he calls houseflies "ladies in black cloaks" and in another decides that a female pig should be dressed up in his mother's clothes. (Puerto Ricans have an expression for a woman who is overdressed: "She looks like the she-pig of Juan Bobo." They've also coined a word for "foolishness" in honor of Juan Bobo — *bobería.*)

Juan Animala is a very different sort of hero, a trickster, a fearless, good-looking, but treacherous guy who is constantly scheming for ways to get money and who somehow always manages to get out of most dangerous adventures scot-free. He particularly enjoys playing outrageous tricks on authority figures.

Juan Cuchilla lacks both the innocence and imagination of Juan Bobo and the shrewd, self-confident independence of Juan Animala. He was born good person, but a lifetime of trouble and misadventures has transformed him into a rogue, a fraud, and a petty thief.

Puerto Rican culture is also filled with dozens of bedtime fairy tales (such as the one introducing this chapter), as well as bogeymen stories guaranteed to frighten even the bravest and most indifferent child.

carefully handed down from generation to generation. Some of these traditions fell by the wayside for a while because younger generations were in a hurry to become part of the mainland's pop culture. Today, in the 1990s, many of these traditions are enjoying a revival as younger generations of Puerto Ricans discover their rich cultural roots. There is one rich folk tradition, however, that has never lost its popularity — Puerto Rican cuisine.

¡Buen Apetito!

It may be hard to find a Puerto Rican restaurant if you do not live in a city with a large Puerto Rican population like New York or Chicago, and there are certainly no fast-food Puerto Rican drive-thrus. But if Puerto Rican cuisine has not yet made the impact on U.S. culture that other ethnic groups have made (like Mexican, Italian, Greek, and Asian Amer-

icans), it is largely because Puerto Ricans have not been living on the mainland as long. They may be hard to find, but the dishes served in Puerto Rican restaurants are well worth the trouble!

The traditions of *cocina criolla*, Puerto Rico's delicious traditional cuisine, date back to the cookery of the original inhabitants of the island, the Arawak, Taino, and Carib Indians. Today's popular barbecue, for example, owes its origin to the ancient Indian version called *barbacoa*. Although this Indian cookery was subsequently enriched with five centuries of Spanish and other European culinary skills, it was the Black slaves brought from Africa to work the sugar fields who had the biggest impact on Puerto Rico's cuisine. Many of the staples of Caribbean diets are foods brought from Africa on the same ships used to transport slaves, foods like coconuts, yams,

Traditional Puerto Rican meals usually feature pork, chicken, or beef, served with a spicy mixture of rice and kidney beans and a side dish of fried or mashed plantains.

millet, sorghum, rice, peanuts, plantains, citrus fruits, cassava, okra, sesame seeds, black-eyed peas, greens, *melegueta* pepper, and palm oil. Africans also brought with them many of their traditional cooking methods.

Puerto Rican cooking differs from other methods of mainland cooking in a number of ways, but the most important is the use of piquant flavorings like fresh lime rind or lime juice, ginger, *naranja agria* (sour orange), cilantro, cumin, oregano, and coriander, to name just a few. The food is rich with spices but not generally "hot" like some of Mexico's jalepeña chili dishes.

There are two particular secret ingredients unique to Puerto Rican dishes: *adobo* and *sofrito*. *Adobo* is a blend of spices (like peppercorns, oregano, garlic cloves, and salt) crushed and mixed together with olive oil and lime juice using a mortar and pestle and then rubbed into poultry and meat several hours before cooking.

Sofrito is a liquid seasoning made by sautéing salt pork, ham, oregano, vegetable oil, onion, green pepper, sweet chili peppers, fresh cilantro leaves, and garlic cloves until they form a liquid. The seasoning can be added to a number of different dishes as flavoring during the cooking process.

BECOMING A NEW YEAR'S FOOL

Part of the special New Year's Eve family dinner is the tradition of dipping for *pasteles*. Each person in turn would fish one of the pasteles right out of the pot they were boiled in with his or her fork. Whoever got the "trick" pastele (the one without stuffing) was the "New Year's Fool."

Another distinction of Puerto Rican cuisine is the use of *achiote* seeds to give a rich orange-red color to traditional rice recipes such as *arroz con pollo,* a delicious kettle dish of browned chicken and rice cooked with peas, olives, chili peppers, onions, diced ham, and tomatoes, and spiced with lime and adobo seasoning.

Rice is the main staple of Puerto Rican cooking. In fact, whether a Puerto Rican is living on the island or in the middle of New York City, dinner is almost always the same: rice, beans, plantains, and some kind of meat. Other savory rice dishes include *arroz con mantequilla y ajo* (rice steamed with butter and garlic) and *asopao de grandules* (seasoned rice with diced ham and pigeon peas).

Dinner can include a variety of beef (*carne*), poultry (*pollo*), and fish (*pescado*) dishes, but pork is a favorite, especially pork chops (*chuletas*). (Unfortunately, this earned the Puerto Ricans who first came to New York the derogatory nickname some Italian Americans gave them of "pork chop.") Particularly tasty are the *carne guisada* (a spicy beef stew) and *lechón asado* (a whole barbecued pig served with plantains and a sour garlic sauce, a traditional dish for outdoor picnics and parties).

Another important staple in Puerto Rican cooking is the plantain, a variety of banana that is never eaten raw but can be fried, roasted, boiled, or baked in a number of delicious recipes. While every Caribbean culture gives plantains their own special twist, Puerto Rican recipes make them especially tasty in a variety of spicy dishes. These include *tostones* (fritters made from peeled and diagonally sliced green plantains that are flattened with a spatula and then fried in hot vegetable oil with garlic and adobe seasoning until golden brown), *pasteles* (a thin layer of plantain batter filled with a spicy ground pork and olive mixture, then rolled up and boiled in plantain leaves, some-

TOSTONES

3 *plátanos verdes* (firm, green plantains)
4 cups water
2 cloves garlic, peeled and
    crushed (optional)
2 tablespoons salt
vegetable oil for frying

Peel plantains and cut into diagonal slices about one inch thick. Add garlic cloves and salt to water. Soak plantain slices for about one-half hour. Drain well (but reserve the water) and then deep-fry in oil (heated to about 350 degrees F) for about seven minutes until plantains are tender but not crusty. Remove from the oil, drain well, then flatten slices with a spatula or the bottom of a drinking glass. Dip each slice in the salted water again, pat dry, then fry again until crusty. Drain on absorbent paper. Makes about twenty-five tostones. (Note: Plantains are available in supermarkets in most large cities.)

what like Mexican *tamales*), *mofongo* (mashed plantains that are seasoned, formed into balls, and deep fried), and *alcapurrias* (a deep-fried, meat-filled, plantain-and-potato mixture).

Red kidney beans *(habichuelas)* cooked in a variety of imaginative and delicious ways make up another staple food. A favorite bean dish that takes three hours to cook is a spicy mixture of red beans, onions, garlic, chili peppers, white wine, and cumin, cooked until thickened, then served in soup bowls with chopped onions sprinkled on top.

In Puerto Rican cuisine, desserts are usually not for everyday meals but are saved for holidays and other special occasions. When desserts are served, they are generally not cakes but creamy custards or puddings, crunchy or chewy cookie squares, crullers, puff pastries, fruit served with syrup, or delicate meringues — and are almost always made with coconut. One dessert that is just as good to smell as it is to eat is *Arroz con Coco*, candied coconut rice flavored with ginger, cloves, nutmeg, and cinnamon. Fruit jellies, preserves, and syrups are

BESITOS DE COCO (COCONUT KISSES)

3 cups grated ripe coconut, firmly
    packed, or 2 cans (4 ounces
    each) of Baker's Southern
    Style Coconut
1 cup brown sugar, firmly packed
8 tablespoons flour
1/4 teaspoon salt
2 ounces (4 tablespoons) butter
4 egg yolks
1/2 teaspoon vanilla extract (or
    grated rind of one lime)

Preheat oven to 350 degrees F. Place grated coconut in a bowl. Add brown sugar, flour, salt, butter, egg yolks, and vanilla (or lime rind). Mix thoroughly. Grease a 13 x 9 x 2 inch glass baking dish. Take mixture by tablespoons, turn into balls, and arrange on baking dish. Bake in preheated oven about thirty to forty minutes, or until golden. Remove from heat and allow to cool, upside down, on a platter. Then, turn over onto another platter for serving.

SHOPPING FOR THE RIGHT PLANTAINS

Plantains can appear bruised and even kind of ugly, ranging anywhere from hard and green to yellow with brown flecks to an almost mushy black. Bu don't let their looks deceive you; these fruits are delicious! If you made the mistake of buying plantains by accident (thinking in your hurry that they were just slightly under-ripe bananas), you would be frustrated to learn, when you got home and tried to eat one, that they were quite hard, difficult to peel, and, well, inedible. That's because plantains are never eaten raw. It is the color of the plantain peel that suggests the best cooking method. The bland, unripe green ones are called *plátanos verdes* and are usually served like boiled potatoes or sliced and added to stews. The yellow ones (only half-ripe) are firm but creamier in texture and taste best baked like a sweet potato, or they can be sautéed, deep-fried, or grilled as an accompaniment to a meat dish. Black plantains, which are ripe and soft, are called *amarillos* and are often used in more elaborate dishes in which they are mashed and combined with other ingredients before cooking. Even the leaves of the plantain serve a useful purpose; they are used to wrap certain foods (such as pasteles) before boiling or baking. Aluminum foil can be substituted, of course, but the flavor is just not the same.

also popular desserts, especially when made with mango, papaya, guava, or plums.

¿Cómo Estás? Puerto Rican Language and Cultural Expressions

Written Spanish is the same in Puerto Rico as it is everywhere else in the world. What makes Puerto Rican Spanish unique are certain pronunciations — and the addition of many Taino and African words. The final *s* on plural endings is often dropped, for example; so is an *s* if it comes before a consonant, as it does in words like *hasta, pasta,* and *este.* The *d* is sometimes silent in words — like *pela(d)o* or *to(d)o* — while, as in other parts of Latin America, *ll* and *y* are pronounced alike (*halla, haya*) and the *v* and *b* are sometimes interchanged (as in *velo* and *bello*). Words derived from African dialects, such as *mambo, gandinga, combo, timba,* and *ganga,* are common in daily language. So are words derived from the language of the Taino, like *hamaca, hiquero, jincho, maguey,* and *guabara.* Many place names on the island are derived from Indian names as well: *Caguas, Guayama, Arecibo,* and *Mayaguez,* for example.

One other way that Puerto Rican Spanish and the Spanish of Spain and other Latin countries differ from one another is in the meanings certain words have acquired in each culture. Not being aware of those differences can be embarrassing. For example, to a Puerto Rican, a *guagua* is a bus, but in Central America, asking for a *guagua* is asking for a baby. (You have to ask for an *autobus* if you want a bus.) In Puerto Rico, if you refer to a *palo,* you are talking about a stick or, in casual settings, a drink; if you refer to a *palo* in Mexico, you are talking about a man's sexual organ. So needless to say, you must be sure you know both your Spanish and your audience.

Christianity is so much a part of daily life for many Puerto Ricans that it even permeates their daily conversation. In planning a matter as casual as meeting for lunch the next day, many Puerto Ricans will add, *"Si Dios quiere"*

("God willing"). Common expressions of surprise are *"Ay virgen!"* and *"Ave Maria!"* both of which refer to the Virgin Mary. Even more frequently used, to express or plead for compassion, is *"Ay bendito!"* which is short for *"Bendito sea El Señor"* ("Blessed be the Lord").

Folk Song and Dance

Puerto Rican music is also a blend of Spanish, African, and native Taino cultures. The first Spaniards may have brought *coplas* (ballads and songs), but it was the Taino who supplied the gourds and maracas and the African slaves who added the distinctive beat of bass drums and bongos and many of the soulful lyrics.

Children's songs are an excellent example of Puerto Rican folk music. Mothers rock their children with traditional lullabies, while older children play sidewalk games while singing story songs like "The Ballad of Angelina," "The Count's Son," "Rice With Milk," and "Alfonso the Twelfth." If a child dies, a traditional song of mourning, called the *baquiné,* is performed at the wake.

Then there are the peasant songs, which range from melancholy ten-stanza *décimas* to festive, danceable *bombeo,* folk ballads accompanied by a guitar or accordion. There are the old songs once sung by peasant washerwomen as they scrubbed clothes in the rivers, the machete songs the men sang together in rhythm while chopping down sugar stalks, or those a man sang by himself when he was leading his ox-drawn plow through a field. Noel Estrada's sentimental ballad, *"En Mi Viejo San Juan"* ("In My Old San Juan") became a favorite with many homesick migrants.

Christmas carols, or *aguinaldos,* are another important form of Puerto Rican folk music. The word *aguinaldo* means a song sung in praise of the Child Jesus in six-syllable verse. Aguinaldos usually combine somber religious sentiment with festive celebration. While they (which also means Christmas gifts offered or received) are most often sung around Christmastide, aguinaldos are not limited to the Christmas cycle and can be sung all year round.

Both the *bomba* and *plena* are exuberant Puerto Rican folk dances that can trace their heritage to Puerto Rico's early African slave population. These musicians are performing the music of these dances at the Central Park bandshell in New York.

Both the music of Puerto Rican folk dance and its traditional costumes — such as these worn in a New York parade — combine Taino Indian, African, and European influences.

Dances have always played a unique and important role in Puerto Rican society. Many diverse styles come under the heading of folk dance music, including *boleros, salsa, cumbia, merenge, tangos,* and traditional *folklorica* music. Not all these Latin styles have strictly Puerto Rican roots. Cumbia, for example, evolved out of a combination of accordion music German immigrants brought to Mexico and Latin folk music — but they are still often part of the repertoire of Puerto Rican musicians.

Like the folk songs, traditional dances had a number of different influences. Some were derived from graceful Spanish dances such as the *matamoros,* in which couples dance separately around each other, turning on their heels; the dizzying *fandango;* and the *sonduro,* for which people danced with metal taps on their shoes, among others. (Some of these dances had strange names such as *Gallinacito, alza que te han visto* — literally, "Little chicken, get up for they've seen you.")

African cultures influenced Puerto Rican music with such sensual and lively dances as the *bomba* (danced to a kettledrum to celebrate the end of the sugar harvest) and the *guateque* (a dance so noisy, frolicky, and agitated that the Puerto Ricans started calling noisy parties *guateques*). African dances like the bomba were often sung by the participants as they danced.

Three major Puerto Rican dance forms developed out of these influences: the *danza,* the *plena,* and the *seis.* The danza, an elegant, formal dance that has been likened to both a minuet and a waltz, emerged in the 1860s and over the years became identified with Puerto Rican nationalism, particularly with the composition of the anthem *"La Borinqueña"* in danza form. The plena, on the other hand, has a strong Afro-Caribbean beat and is less refined and more exuberant. It is said to have originated after World War I in the dives and bar rooms of Ponce, but it became acceptable to general Puerto Rican society when the well-known folksinger Manuel Jimenez Otero popularized it several years later. The third major folk dance form, the seis, is an expressive dance with a Creole spirit that is performed with many variations.

We will discuss some of the important Puerto Rican contributions to the current American music scene (in genres such as pop, jazz, rock, and hip hop) in the next chapter.

Winter Baseball: A League with Tradition

Puerto Ricans have a passion for baseball and, as we will see in the next chapter, have contributed some very talented ball players to the mainland's major league teams. The passion is not just for the National and American Leagues, however. Puerto Ricans on the island and the mainland alike are also avid followers of winter baseball in the Puerto Rican League, where Latin players turn out in great numbers to stay in shape and keep their skills sharp for summer on the mainland.

No one gets rich playing baseball in Puerto Rico. The Puerto Rican League has a maximum player salary of five thousand dollars per month. But this is not minor league baseball, and every team in the league fields at least four or five Puerto Rican major league stars. Puerto Rican and other Latin major leaguers want to play here for a variety of reasons. For one thing, most grew up playing baseball year-round. And Puerto Rican major leaguers want to give back something to their homeland, to let their fans, many of whom will never get to the States, see their heroes in person.

Past and present Puerto Rican major league stars who have excited their fans on the island and mainland alike include Ruben Sierra, Sandy Alomar, Sr., Sandy Alomar, Jr., Joey Cora, Carlos Baerga, Juan Gonzalez, Bernie Williams, José Santiago, Roberto Alomar, Edgar Martinez, Carlos Delgado, José Valentin, Orlando Cepeda, and one of the all-time greatest names in all of baseball, Roberto Clemente.

Most Puerto Ricans are avid sports fans, whether they are young or old, male or female, player or participant — and whether they live on the island or the mainland.

The Puerto Rican League, in operation since 1938, can boast some famous non-Puerto Rican names as well, like Willie Mays, Hank Aaron, and Sandy Koufax. Whether or not Negro League stars ever reached the U.S. big leagues after Jackie Robinson integrated them when he broke in with the Brooklyn Dodgers in the 1940s, such Negro League stars as Roy Campanella (who eventually became a mainstay with the Dodgers), Luke Easter, Josh Gibson, Buck Leonard, and Satchel Paige were always welcome in the Puerto Rican League.

Whether the field is sports, music, art, language, literature, or food, the Puerto Rican influence on mainland culture has been strong and, as new generations of Puerto Ricans rediscover their rich folk heritage, that influence is getting even stronger.

Brothers Roberto and Sandy Alomar, shown here warming up with the American League All-Stars in 1991, are among the many Puerto Rican baseball players who have graced the major leagues with their talents and their enthusiasm for the game.

CHAPTER SIX

CONTRIBUTIONS TO AMERICAN CULTURE
SUBSTANCE AND STYLE FOR THE MAINSTREAM

According to *Billboard* magazine, in 1990 Latin music was an $80 million industry in the United States. By 1995, that figure had doubled and continues to grow at a fantastic rate. Latin music has also profoundly influenced almost every other genre of American music — jazz, blues, dance music, and pop — and now it is even on the cutting edge of rock 'n' roll. And like Puerto Ricans in so many other walks of life on the U.S. mainland, Puerto Rican musicians are playing an active role in this success.

Puerto Ricans and the Latin Music Scene

Among some of the most notable Latin pop stars with Puerto Rican roots have been singers José Feliciano, Tony Orlando, Danny Rivera, Chayanne, and Ednita Nazario, and the singing group Menudo. One of the most popular balladeers on Latin pop radio in the nineties has been Julian, a German-born, San Francisco-raised artist whose Puerto Rican parents give him his Latin ancestry. Although it is not easy for a Latin singer to cross over to the U.S. pop charts, Julian is fluent in both English and Spanish and records his songs in both languages, a move that has gained him widespread recognition, not just in the United States, but internationally.

Mainstream dance music has also had its share of Latin influence with Latin dances like the rumba, mambo, samba, merengue, and even the lambada of the early 1990s. Salsa did not really become popular on the U.S. mainland until the 1970s, although it dates back to the eighteenth century, when the songs and rhythms that African slaves brought with them to Caribbean sugar plantations combined with traditional Spanish folk music. Salsa instrumentation features piano, brass, percussion (such as conga drums, or timbales) and some-

Puerto Rican singer, guitarist, and pop recording star José Feliciano gained mainstream popularity in the 1970s.

LIGHT MY FIRE

Singer-guitarist José Feliciano became a pop recording star in the summer of 1968 with his Latin-soul version of the Doors' "Light My Fire." That same year, he was awarded two Grammys — one for best male pop singer and the other for best new artist of the year. Feliciano, who was born blind because of glaucoma, moved from Puerto Rico to New York with his parents when he was five. By the time he was in his late teens, he had taught himself to play six- and twelve-string guitars, the bass, mandolin, piano, drums, harpsichord, harmonica, and trumpet, and he was performing in coffee houses in Greenwich Village. He recorded his first solo album in 1966 but did not really become well known outside of the Latino community until he sang his unorthodox and moving blues-rock rendition of "The Star Spangled Banner" at the opening of the fifth game of the 1968 baseball World Series in Detroit's Tiger Stadium.

times even flutes and violins, as well as a lead singer.

The steady, two-part beat makes the music compellingly danceable. By 1930, East Harlem, New York, had developed a flourishing salsa musical culture with clubs such as the Teatro San José on 110th Street and the Teatro Hispano on 116th. As Latin music caught on,

IN LOVE WITH A TALL, DARK STRANGER

On the U.S. mainland, dances like the tango, rumba, mambo, and conga really belonged more to Hollywood than to Puerto Ricans and other Latinos. When an Italian actor named Rudolph Valentino dressed as a gaucho and danced the tango on the silver screen, he sent non-Hispanic women into spasms of sighing. After all, as a "Latin," Valentino was the perfect erotic fantasy: the tall, dark stranger whose every move was mysterious and seductive. (Lupe Velez and Dolores del Rio, who actually *were* Latinas, were Valentino's female counterparts in darkened U.S. theaters.) Like Valentino, actor Van Johnson was not Latino, but it was he who helped popularize the conga line and made it the perfect party dance.

Hollywood fans also liked their Latin music whimsical and a bit outrageous, as well. Cuban bandleader Xavier Cugat often appeared on screen with his absurd pet Chihuahua, and dancer/singer Carmen Miranda — billed as "the Brazilian Bombshell" — nearly always showed up with a salad of fresh fruit on her head.

By the fifties, "Latin" was definitely in. Latin nightclubs were opening all over New York and Chicago, and society matrons were considered chic only if they carried a tiny Chihuahua or two in their mink-draped arms. Male musicians and dancers decked out with ruffled sleeves and maracas, Van Johnson-style, were the rage at nightclubs everywhere, and suburban couples were scrambling to take rumba lessons at their local Arthur Murray dance studio.

In spite of its popularity on the mainland, however, Latin dance music remained the music of "foreigners" to most non-Hispanic Americans.

Puerto Rican bandleader and percussionist Tito Puente, a mainstay of the Latin music scene for decades, has long appealed to fans of many musical stripes. In the early days of his career, he wowed non-Hispanic audiences in many Harlem clubs and recently appeared in the movie *Mambo Kings*.

Puerto Rican and other Latin musicians were making appearances with their own bands in Harlem clubs such the Savoy Ballroom, the Apollo Theater, and the Paladium Dance Hall.

A relatively new genre in mainland Latino music — but possibly the fastest growing one — is Latin rock, a crashing, nervous music filled with piercing vocals, thundering guitars, and rolling drums. It combines the Jamaican strains of reggae and ska and draws on the influences of both U.S. and British rock bands.

Latin rock started out as a Latin American phenomenon, but by the mid-1990s, Latino kids in the United States were starting to plug into the sound, too. The major reason was *MTV Latino*. In addition to its 260-million-viewer audience throughout Latin America, the Miami-based cable channel started broadcasting its music programming into U.S. cities as far north as Chicago.

Although rap and hip hop are generally considered African American music genres, Latino groups like Cypress Hill have been on the scene since the early nineties, dressing up rap music by giving an electronic hip hop beat a touch of reggae or merengue and then filtering it through saxophone riffs. While the hard-edged lyrics that often deal with violence, rage, and sex do not exactly reflect the love and romance that have long been the traditional themes of Latin music, *el rap* does have strong roots in the storytelling tradition of the Puerto Rican street poets of the 1950s and in the vocal harmonization of the doo-wop groups of that time. Some of the hottest Puerto Rican rappers of the nineties include singer Lisa M, who mixes rap and reggae with a sultry rock ballad style, and Vico-C, who adds mambo and flamenco rhythms to his rapping chants.

LOS SANTEROS

When the Spanish first arrived in Puerto Rico and started building Catholic churches and cathedrals, they could not import enough statues and other religious images to properly decorate them, so they did the next best thing: They commissioned local artisans to carve religious statues out of native mahogany and cedar. These artisans came to be known as *Los Santeros,* or saint-carvers, and woodcarving became a specialty that was handed down from father to son. The santeros rarely signed their work or received any other credit besides a small payment, but today the art they created is eagerly sought by collectors and exhibited in museums throughout the world.

On a More Serious Note . . .

Throughout its history, jazz, that most American of musical forms, jazz, has been energized by Puerto Rican musicians like the famous jazz trombonist Juan Tizol, who played with Duke Ellington during his orchestra's heyday in the 1930s and 1940s. Puerto Ricans have made tremendous contributions to classical music, too. Internationally renowned Puerto Rican opera singer Justino Díaz has played a wide range of leading bass roles in such prestigious opera houses as the Metropolitan in New York, where he made his debut in 1963; La Scala in Milan, Italy; the Hamburg State Opera in Germany; and Covent Garden in London.

Other famous Puerto Rican opera stars include Ester Comas, Graciela Rivera, and Martina Arroyo. Classical musicians from Puerto Rico who have achieved world recognition include classical guitarists William San-taella and Leo Rivera and violinist José Figueroa.

In classical dance, Puerto Rican dancers Brunhilda Ruiz and Edward Villella have achieved worldwide recognition in ballet. Villella helped introduce a dynamic new masculine style to classical ballet. Instead of playing the traditional secondary role of supporting the ballerina, he created a role that was vigorous, virile, athletic, and self-assertive. His spectacular style was enthusiastically received and has helped influence a whole generation of modern and classical dancers. Tina Ramirez, another Puerto Rican dancer and teacher, has made the Ballet Hispanico of New York a thriving and prestigious dance company.

Painting and Sculpture

Puerto Rican artists have always had a rich cultural heritage to draw on and that is more true today than ever. Spanish religious painting and carving and the influences of African and Taino folk art often combine with formal Western European training and the vivid urban environment of the Barrio to create an impressive artistic expression of Puerto Rican insight and feeling. Many Puerto Rican artists (like Dennis Mario Rivera) who now work in New York often continue to commute, physically and artistically, between the island and the mainland. They also often find inspiration in other Caribbean cultures.

Examples of highly esteemed contemporary Puerto Rican artists include Roberto Lebrón, Ramón Carrasquillo, Rafael Ferrer, and Wilfred Labrosa.

One organization that has set out to keep alive the knowledge and interest in the visual arts among Puerto Ricans has been the Museo del Barrio in New York City. It is a showcase where Puerto Rican artists young and old, known and unknown, can achieve recognition

DENNIS MARIO RIVERA: COMMITTED TO ART AND TO LIFE

The kinetic lines and electric colors Puerto Rican artist (and musician) Dennis Mario Rivera uses to paint his enlarged canvases seem to jump out at the viewer with the same vibrant energy as the music he plays. In the paintings created for his 1995 show at the Smithsonian's Anacostia Museum in Washington, D.C. ("Afro-Caribe: The Art of Dennis Mario Rivera"), thirty-seven-year-old Rivera traced his African roots and their influence on his Caribbean island homeland, Puerto Rico. "I try to study different expres-

sions of the black heritage in the Americas. We all come from the same thing, the blackness of the motherland Africa," the artist explains. Rivera is also strongly committed to human-rights causes and the fight for Puerto Rican independence, a stance that has often earned him the reputation of a rabble-rouser — and, as a result, few invitations to exhibit in Puerto Rico. His artistic message to the world is a simple but powerful one: Be true to yourself, be true to your heritage, and be human.

for their talents. Other efforts to promote the arts in New York have been supported by the Friends of Puerto Rico and the Institute of Contemporary Hispanic Arts.

Literature

Starting in the early 1930s, talented Puerto Rican writers like Antonio Pedreira, René Marquéz, Miguel Algarín, Edmundo Rivera

Alvarez, and Enrique Laguerre have written dramatically about the themes of migration, the displacement of the *jíbaro* (a member of Puerto Rico's landless, tenant-farmer class), and the difficulties and challenges of living in an often prejudiced urban society. Plays like *Tiempo Muerto,* by Méndez Ballester, have been another powerful vehicle in dealing with these themes. By the 1950s, Puerto Rican writers

DOWN THESE MEAN STREETS

Second-generation mainland Puerto Ricans often experienced more of an identity crisis in New York City than their parents did. Gifted Puerto Rican writers like Piri Thomas have written brutal and vivid descriptions of what it was like to grow up in an environment of intense prejudice and poverty.

Although Piri Thomas was born into a stable, upwardly mobile family that eventually moved out of the slums and bought a home on Long Island, Piri himself became lost. In his autobiography, *Down These Mean Streets*, he tells how he was introduced to

the gang life of East Harlem and with it, sex, drugs, and thievery — and eventually more serious crimes. Part of the book deals with his struggles with addiction, but the central issue for Piri was color.

Piri is what Puerto Ricans call *trigueño* (the "color of wheat"), but his hostile New York world saw (and treated) him as Black. Throughout the book, his angry struggles against prejudice, violence, and discrimination continued to torture him. First published in 1967, *Down These Mean Streets* has become a modern literary classic.

of the second mainland generation like Piri Thomas had begun to write in English as well as Spanish.

Prominent contemporary Puerto Rican writers include Jesús Colón, Miguel Algarín, J. L. Torres, Ed Vega, Judith Ortíz-Cofer, Nicholasa Mohr, playwright René Marquéz, journalist Pablo Guzmán, and Chicago poet David Hernández.

Stage and Screen

Until recently, Puerto Rican characters were rarely featured in major film roles. When they were, they were usually depicted with the same stereotypes that other Latinos (particularly Mexican Americans) have had to endure. These stereotypes date back to the early days of cinema and such so-called "greaser" films as *Bronco Billy and the Greaser* (produced in 1914). This movie was one of the first to use the "bandit" stereotype: Latins as dirty, unkempt, unshaven, violent, irrational criminals.

Another standard Latin American stereotype has been the "buffoon," usually the comic sidekick of the Anglo hero, a loveable simpleton who is somewhat backward or not quite ready to assimilate into respectable Anglo-American society (like Pancho in "The Cisco Kid" or Ricky Ricardo in "I Love Lucy"). The female buffoon character is usually a dizzy, sexy-but-dumb spitfire type, like the characters with elaborate fruit hats played by Carmen Miranda.

Until the mid-1980s, the only movies that even tried to deal with real Hispanic American issues were the bleak social melodramas of the fifties and early sixties about worker exploitation and youth gangs. Even these well-meaning (but patronizing) films had a hard time staying away from stereotypes. For example, updated versions of the *bandido* stereotype can be found in *West Side Story* (a 1961 musical tragedy about violent Puerto Rican gang members) and *The Young Savages* (a 1961

Puerto Rican actress Chita Rivera received the 1993 Tony Award for best performance by a leading actress in a musical for her performance in "Kiss of the Spider Woman."

courtroom drama about a seemingly innocent Puerto Rican teen who was murdered by Italian American gang members). Even movies made as late as the 1980s (like *Raiders of the Lost Ark* and *Romancing the Stone*) showed Anglo heroes menaced by all sorts of corrupt and despicable Latino bad-guy types.

By the 1980s, a number of talented Puerto Ricans and other Latinos had emerged on the Hollywood scene. They began working behind the camera as writers, producers, and directors, creating films that exploded the old stereotypes and started dealing realistically with Hispanic American issues. A good example is Puerto Rican director Leon Ichaso's *Crossover Dreams* (1984), the story about an ambitious New York salsa musician who turned his back on his Latino friends and his barrio roots to achieve mainstream success but failed to make it and returned instead to his old neighborhood to reaffirm the traditional Latino values he was raised by.

WEST SIDE STORY: THE MODERN ROMEO AND JULIET

Puerto Ricans were not often the subject of works of U.S. culture — until 1957, when a musical drama about Puerto Rican teens in New York City became a smash Broadway hit. *West Side Story,* a modern version of Shakespeare's *Romeo and Juliet,* is a tragic story about two young lovers, a Puerto Rican girl named Maria and a white boy named Tony, who get caught between the rivalry of two feuding street gangs in New York's Hell's Kitchen. Puerto Rican actress Chita Rivera was nominated for a Tony Award for her portrayal of Maria's friend Anita. The musical was later made into a movie for which Puerto Rican actress Rita Moreno won an Oscar for best supporting actress.

Puerto Rican actress Rita Moreno, shown here in a dance number, won an Oscar for her role as Anita in the movie version of *West Side Story*, a Broadway musical about love and life in America for members of a New York Puerto Rican gang.

Puerto Rican actor Erik Estrada starred as a police officer in the 1978 TV show "CHiPs."

Puerto Ricans have had a bit more success in front of the camera over the years, although actors, too, have often had to fight for a chance at mainstream stardom. Four particularly dramatic Puerto Rican stage and screen success stories have been Puerto Rican-born actor-director José Ferrer, Broadway song-and-dance actresses Chita Rivera and Rita Moreno, and Broadway and film star Raul Julia.

Other movie and television personalities who are of Puerto Rican descent include Liz Torres (of TV's "Larroquette" show), Eric Estrada ("CHiPs"), Jimmy Smitz ("L.A. Law" and "NYPD Blue"), Esai Morales (the movie *La Bamba),* Vanna White ("Wheel of Fortune"), talk-show host Geraldo Rivera, and the late Freddie Prinz ("Chico and the Man").

Theater

Puerto Ricans developed a passionate interest in the theater in the nineteenth century, when famous musicians, opera singers, orchestras, and dramatic companies made frequent appearances in the island's larger cities and often even in smaller towns. Fine arts lovers organized literary soirees and other activities to get people involved in good music, theater, opera, and poetry. Theater companies were formed that not only performed contemporary productions but kept alive the traditional folk theater of Puerto Rico as well. Many, such as New York's Puerto Rican Traveling Theater, are still thriving today.

Best known as a gameshow hostess on "Wheel of Fortune," Vanna White also starred as Venus, goddess of love, in a 1988 made-for-TV romantic comedy.

LATINOS BEAM INTO THE *STAR TREK* UNIVERSE

In the mid-1990s, creators of the ongoing TV series *Star Trek* changed the program's format to include a sleek, new ship, a female captain, and a multicultural starship crew featuring not one, but two Latino actors as leading characters.

Robert Beltran, a Mexican American actor, portrays first officer Chakotay, and Roxann Biggs-Dawson, a fourth-generation U.S. Puerto Rican born and raised in Los Angeles, plays B'Elanna Torres. The character Torres is the *Voyager's* highly capable, half-Latina human, half-Klingon chief engineer who despises her brutal, angry Klingon side and must constantly struggle to keep her emotions in check.

Although the multicultural crew was meant to represent the world as it could and should be in the twenty-fourth century, it has raised issues that are relevant to our day. Some couch-potato critics actually griped that with a female captain, a half-Klingon/half-Latina chief engineer, a Native American first officer, a Black Vulcan, a Latino first officer, an Asian American crew member, and a holographic doctor (among others), the producers of *Star Trek* had gone too far and taken "political correctness" to its extreme.

Radio

Programs on mainstream radio featuring Latin music have been popular ever since New York's El Barrio had its own music show broadcast over WABC radio in the thirties. The weekly program was hosted by Julio Roque, an East Harlem dentist and musician who played both the traditional Puerto Rican plenas and the popular Latin salsa music played by bands like that of Tito Rodriguez.

Since 1993, National Public Radio has been airing an hour-long weekly program called "*Club del Sol*" to present such musical rhythms of the Americas as merengue, tango, mariachi, cumbia, ranchera, samba, and many others. The program is hosted by popular Puerto Rican jazz flutist Dave Valentin, whose expertise includes traditional Caribbean music, Afro-Caribbean styles, and the folk idioms of the Andes. The show features a mix of live performances recorded in the United States as well as the recordings of Latin music superstars like Tito Puente, Gilberto Gil, Astor Piazzolla, and Poncho Sánchez.

Sports

As we have seen in Chapter Five, Puerto Rico has made two tremendous contributions to American baseball: talented major league players and a winter league where U.S. ball players can stay in shape between seasons.

Of course, baseball has not been Puerto Rico's only contribution to sports excellence. Carlos Ortiz, a Puerto Rican-born New Yorker, won the lightweight boxing championship twice — once by defeating Joe Brown in 1962, and then, after losing the championship to Ismael Laguna in 1965, regaining it from him again that same year. Another championship Puerto Rican boxer was Sixto Escobar, who, at 5'4" and 118 pounds, held the professional bantamweight title three different times and was never knocked down in his sixty-four fights. He finally gave up boxing in 1939 (when he could no longer meet the 118-pound weight requirement) and was voted into the Boxing Hall of Fame in 1975.

Juan A. "Chi Chi" Rodriguez has what is considered to be one of the most powerful

Puerto Rican boxer Sixto Escobar held the pro bantamweight title three different times before he ended his boxing career in 1939.

Puerto Rican pro golfer Chi Chi Rodriguez has been one of the century's most beloved golf heroes.

swings in professional golf, despite his relatively small size — 5' 7" and 130 pounds. In twenty-five years on the PGA tour, Rodriguez won eight tournaments and more than 1 million dollars. In 1985, he joined the Senior Tour (for those of age fifty and over) and has won more tournaments (and more money) since then than he did on the regular pro tour. In his book *Chi Chi's Secret of Power Golf* (1967), he explained how his special stance helped him outdistance much bigger and stronger pros.

Other outstanding Puerto Rican sports stars include tennis great GiGi Fernández, Olympic swimmer Chayenne Vasallo, and one of the most successful horse jockeys in U.S. history — Angel Cordero.

Commonwealth or Statehood? A Look to the Future

An important issue for Puerto Ricans living on the island is the question of whether Puerto Rico should become the fifty-first U.S. state, continue to be a commonwealth of the United States, or seek outright independence. (If Puerto Ricans decide that they want to become a state, their decision still has to be ratified by the U.S. Congress.)

Puerto Ricans have been grappling with these choices ever since their island was taken over by the United States in 1898. At that time, Puerto Rico was desperately poor and heavily dependent on one crop — sugar. Today, with its solid industrial base, the island is relatively prosperous, particularly compared to other

ROBERTO CLEMENTE: HERO AND LEGEND

For both his outstanding achievements as a professional baseball player and for in involvement in community activities, Roberto Clemente has become, perhaps, the most beloved hero of Puerto Ricans everywhere. He was recruited by the Santurce baseball team of the Puerto Rican League when he was just seventeen. Four years later, in 1955, his outstanding .356 batting average captured the attention of major league scouts, and he was signed by the Pittsburgh Pirates. In his eighteen seasons with that team, Clemente played in twelve All-Star games, won four National League batting championships, claimed a lifetime batting average of .317, and earned the Gold Glove Award for outstanding fielding eleven times.

Just as outstanding was Clemente's record of community achievement. He took great pride in his Puerto Rican heritage and spent much of his time involved in special charity projects there. "If you have the opportunity to make things better, and you don't do that," he said in a speech in 1971, "you are wasting your time on this earth." He was working on a "sports city" project for Puerto Rican children when he was tragically killed in a plane crash off the coast of San Juan on December 31, 1972, while attempting to deliver supplies to earthquake victims in Nicaragua. He was only thirty-eight. Clemente was inducted into the Baseball Hall of Fame the following year, the first Latino player to receive this honor.

countries in the Caribbean. In fact, if you can ignore the island's tropical sunshine and the colonial splendors of Old San Juan and concentrate instead on the freeways, skyscrapers, and crowded downtown shopping areas, you can imagine yourself almost anywhere in the United States.

Puerto Rico's special form of colonial relationship with the United States (politely known as "commonwealth status") was introduced in 1952 by the island's first elected Puerto Rican governor, Luis Muñoz Marín. This relationship has brought Puerto Ricans all the advantages of attachment to the United States — citizenship, the U.S. dollar, a common market — without the burden of federal taxes. Furthermore, as citizens of a commonwealth, Puerto Ricans have kept their cultural independence. They have even kept many of their national symbols and representatives in the international arena, such as the Puerto Rican Olympic team (the island has a tremendous number of sports fans) and their own entrants to international beauty competitions (three of the reigning Miss Universes in the last twenty years have been Puerto Rican). Above all, Puerto Ricans preserved their national identity by holding on to their Spanish language and the idea of nationhood that it represents.

The Popular Democrats, the political party that supports maintaining Puerto Rico's commonwealth status, claims that statehood would just bring on more taxes. Its followers also believe that statehood would mean an end to special tax breaks for mainland-owned corporations. This would, in turn, cause the disappearance of more than half of the three hundred thousand or so jobs that these companies have directly or indirectly created in Puerto Rico. Commonwealth supporters claim to be the majority of Puerto Ricans on the island.

But the "statehooders" also claim to be in the majority. Members of the New Progressive Party (led by reform-minded governor Pedro Rossello) agree that the commonwealth might have worked for the first twenty years since 1952, but insist that it has not worked a all for the past twenty years or so. The standard of living in Puerto Rico, they say, should be compared not with poorer Caribbean nations, like Haiti, but with U.S. states, like Hawaii and Mississippi: Income per head in Puerto Rico remains about at about one-third that of the U.S. average, roughly where it was in 1970.

Statehooders argue that Puerto Ricans have little to lose except their continuing high unemployment (18 percent) and bloated government bureaucracy (22 percent of all employed islanders work for the government). True, Puerto Ricans would have to pay federal taxes, but they would get money back from Washington in the form of increases in such services as food stamps, Medicaid, and other federal programs. They also point out that Congress is already beginning to scale down the special tax breaks it previously offered mainland companies to operate on the island. Only if Puerto Rico became a U.S. state, they argue, would businesses, money, and tourists continue to flock to the island because the costs of wages and services are still well below the U.S. average. And with statehood, Puerto Rico would at last have some political clout, with two U.S. senators and six to eight U.S. representatives for its 3.6 million people (instead of the single nonvoting member of the House it has at present).

Even if Puerto Ricans agree to push for statehood, the question of whether Congress would happily go along with the idea is another matter. Some mainland politicians worry about the financial burdens statehood would impose on the federal government and about the effect it would have on Washington's political balance. (Puerto Rico's congressional delegation would, it is assumed, be mostly Democratic.) Some even worry that if Puerto Rico were granted statehood, the District of Columbia (which has also been dissatisfied with its lack of congressional representation) would insist on being granted statehood as well. And others, who have consistently opposed bilingualism in the United States even on the relatively small level of local school districts, have deep misgivings about having an entire state whose primary language is Spanish.

In addition to the two main movements (statehood vs. commonwealth status), there is the small but vocal independence movement led by Ruben Berrios. Although they only have the support of 5 percent of the Puerto Rican voters (at most), independence advocates believe they can win anyway. They rest their hopes on a series of events, beginning with statehooders' eventually gaining a powerful enough majority for the island to officially choose to become a state. Members of the independence movement believe that if state-

hood wins out, Congress will decide that Puerto Rican statehood is not in the mainland's best interest and will vote it down. At that point, they are sure that Puerto Ricans will be so angry at the decision that they will prefer Puerto Rican independence to remaining a U.S. commonwealth.

When Puerto Ricans voted on the matter in 1967, they endorsed maintaining the commonwealth by a large margin. In a 1993 referendum, the vote was almost evenly divided between those promoting statehood and those promoting commonwealth status. (Independence supporters received only about 4 percent of the vote.)

Whether or not Puerto Rico decides to become the fifty-first U.S. state — and whether that choice is then accepted in Washington, D.C. — both island and mainland Puerto Ricans continue to enrich every facet of U.S. culture. And with their strong family ties, spiritual beliefs, and faith in community activism, Puerto Ricans have long embodied the highest and most admirable of American values.

These scouts parade with both U.S. and Puerto Rican symbols. Many Puerto Ricans favor statehood for their island homeland, others prefer it stay a commonwealth, and a few favor independence. But even those who are most enthusiastically "American" take great pride in their cultural heritage and traditions.

CHRONOLOGY

300 B.C. -A.D. 800 The spread of Arawak-speaking groups throughout the Lesser Antilles, Puerto Rico, and the other islands of the Greater Antilles, where they introduce slash-and-burn agriculture and pottery making.

800-1493 Evolution of Taino culture and society in Puerto Rico (and the other islands of the Greater Antilles); agricultural productivity grows; society becomes more complex; population grows; aggressive Carib groups migrate from northern South America to Puerto Rico and the Lesser Antilles.

1493 Christopher Columbus happens upon the Taino island of Boriquén and names it San Juan Bautista. (Later the island becomes known as Puerto Rico.)

1503 The Spanish Crown of Castille authorizes the shipping of African slaves to the Americas.

1509 The first African slaves arrive in Puerto Rico.

1511 Taino inhabitants launch their first rebellion against the Spanish; the rebellion is crushed, and many Taino flee to neighboring islands.

1565 The last Taino rebellion against the Spanish is crushed.

1625 A Dutch expedition attacks and takes the city of San Juan; after occupying the city for two months, the Dutch burn most of it and then sail away.

1797 The British attack Puerto Rico but are forced to withdraw; Spain authorizes trade between Puerto Rico and neutral powers.

1810 Wars of independence get underway on the Spanish American mainland.

1826 At a congress of American republics, Simón Bolívar advocates creation of an army to liberate Puerto Rico and Cuba; the U.S. opposes the plan.

1838 Buenaventura Quiñones and others plan an uprising to proclaim Puerto Rican independence; the plan is discovered and they are arrested.

1845 Spain finally gives in to British pressure and puts an end to the Black slave trade in Puerto Rico.

1848 Slave rebellions in Puerto Rico lead Spanish Governor Juan Prim to issue the *Bando Negro*.

1865 Cuban and Puerto Rican separatists establish a pro-independence Republican Society in New York City.

1868 Pro-independence groups take over Lares and proclaim the creation of the Republic of Puerto Rico.

1869 Spain grants Puerto Rico the right to elect deputies to the Spanish Cortes.

1873 Slavery is abolished in Puerto Rico.

1892 The Cuban Revolutionary Party is founded in New York City; a Puerto Rican Section of the party is organized.

1893 Working-class Puerto Ricans living in New York City begin to organize.

1897 Spain grants Puerto Rico an Autonomous Charter.

1898 The United States goes to war against Spain; by September, Spain cedes Puerto Rico to the United States.

1900 The Foraker Act sets up civil government; Charles A. Allen becomes the first civilian governor under U.S. colonial rule.

1917 The United States enters World War I and passes the Jones Act, which imposes U.S. citizenship on Puerto Ricans and makes them subject to U.S. draft laws.

1918 The U.S. declares Puerto Rico an "unincorporated territory" belonging to but not forming part of the U.S.

1928   The Depression hits Puerto Rico; by 1930, 36 percent of the employable inhabitants are out of work.

1932   Santiago Iglesias is elected Resident Commissioner to Washington.

1933-34 Sugar cane workers in Puerto Rico go on strike.

1935   Nationalist militants are killed by the police at the University of Puerto Rico.

1937   Police open fire on a Nationalist Party parade in Ponce ("The Ponce Massacre").

1940   Luis Muñoz Marín is elected president of island's senate.

1946   President Truman names Jesús T. Piñero the first Puerto Rican governor of the island; the post-WWII migration of Puerto Ricans to the mainland begins.

1947   "Operation Bootstrap" goes into effect to attract foreign investors; Truman signs the Cutler-Butler Act, permitting Puerto Ricans to elect their own governor.

1948   Students at the University of Puerto Rico go on strike; Luis Muñoz Marín becomes the first elected governor in Puerto Rico's history.

1952   The first constitution of the Commonwealth of Puerto Rico is ratified.

1954   March 1: Puerto Rican Nationalists open fire in the U.S. House of Representatives, wounding five.

1962   Muñoz Marín and President John F. Kennedy arrange for the creation of a joint U.S.-Puerto Rico Status Commission to conduct studies on the status of the island.

1973   The National Guard is called up to run companies immobilized by massive island strikes; University of Puerto Rico closes when students strike.

1975   President Gerald Ford issues a declaration supporting statehood for Puerto Rico.

1979   Inflation rate on the island is at 30 percent and growing; unemployment is at 20-40 percent; inhabitants step up their campaign to get the U.S. Navy to stop using the island for shelling and bombing practice and for storage of bombs and other explosives.

1993   In an island referendum, Puerto Ricans vote for statehood, continued commonwealth status, or independence; the vote was almost evenly divided between those for statehood (46 percent) and those for continued commonwealth status (48 percent); independence supporters received only about 4 percent of the vote; nothing was decided because none of the three options received the required 50 percent.

GLOSSARY

Antojos   Unusual cravings a woman has when pregnant.

Barrio   An urban Puerto Rican neighborhood.

Bodega   A neighborhood grocery store.

Botanica   A neighborhood boutique selling magical and spiritual paraphernalia.

Brujería   Witchcraft.

Compadrazgo   Godparenthood or special friendship.

Compadres   Godparents or very close friends.

Danza	An elegant, formal dance with a strong Afro-Caribbean beat.
El Barrio	"The Neighborhood"; the Puerto Rican community along New York's East 116th Street, also known as Spanish Harlem.
Espiritismo	Spiritism, a religious practice rooted in the belief that people in this world can establish contact with the spirit world and can then use this power for good or evil.
Haciendas	Large farms owned by wealthy landowners and farmed by generation after generation of poor, landless tenants.
Intranquil spirits	In spiritism, the spirits of the recently departed who get stuck hovering a few inches above the earth, spending their time interfering with the lives of the living.
Jíbaros	Poor, landless tenant farmers (also called *agregados*).
Machismo	The dominance of males; a traditional social system in which the man is the breadwinner and the protector of his family, while the woman is brought up to serve her husband, raise devout children, and keep a spotless house.
Mesa Blanca	A religious belief system that calls on the power of saints.
Nuyoricans	What many Puerto Ricans living in New York City choose to call themselves.
Pasteles	A spicy ground pork and olive mixture rolled in batter and boiled in plantain leaves; somewhat like Mexican tamales.
Plantain	A variety of banana that can be fried, roasted, boiled, or baked in a number of delicious recipes.
Promesas	Promises made to God by widows, orphans, mothers, or other relatives of someone recently deceased, like vowing to wear black or never to cut their hair for the rest of their lives.
Salsa	A Caribbean dance with a lead singer and steady beat, often played with congas or timbales.
Santería	A religious belief system that calls on the power of saints and African deities called *orishas*.
Taino	Indians who inhabited the island since before Spanish colonists arrived in the early 1500s.
Velario	A wake; the period of time after a person's death during which the corpse remains in the family home overnight and people are permitted to come and pay their respects.

FURTHER READING

Alegria, Ricardo E. *The Three Wishes: A Collection of Puerto Rican Folktales.* New York: Harcourt, Brace and World, 1969.

Candelaria, Nash. *The Day the Cisco Kid Shot John Wayne.* Tempe, Arizona: Bilingual Press, 1988.

Chavez, Linda. *Out of the Barrio.* New York: Basic Books, 1991.

Colón, Jesús. *A Puerto Rican in New York and Other Sketches.* New York: International Publishers, 1982.

Mohr, Nicholasa. *Rituals of Survival: a Woman's Portfolio.* Houston: Arte Publico Press, 1985.

Murphy, Joseph M. *Santería.* Boston: Beacon Press, 1988.

Ortiz Cofer, Judith. *Silent Dancing: a Partial Remembrance of a Puerto Rican Childhood.* Houston: Arte Publico Press, 1990.

Thomas, Piri. *Down These Mean Streets.* New York: Alfred A. Knopf, 1967.

Valldejuli, Carmen Aboy. *Puerto Rican Cookery.* Gretna, Louisiana: Pelican Publishing, 1994.

Vega, Ed. *The Comeback.* Houston: Arte Publico Press, 1985.

INDEX